DESIGN PROTECTION

a guide to the law
on plagiarism for
manufacturers and
designers

Dan Johnston

illustrations by Peter Kneebone

Design Council

Design Protection
a guide to the law on plagiarism for
manufacturers and designers

First edition published in the United Kingdom 1978 by
Design Council
28 Haymarket   London SW1Y 4SU

Typesetting by
Burgess & Son (Abingdon) Ltd   Abingdon

Printed and bound in the United Kingdom by
A Wheaton & Co Ltd   Exeter

Distributed in the United Kingdom by
Heinemann Educational Books Ltd
48 Charles Street   London W1X 8AH

ISBN 0 85072 088 5

CONTENTS

Acknowledgements

As the author, I accept full responsibility for the explanations and opinions given in this book, but I gratefully acknowledge the help and advice given by the following friends and organisations.

Michael Edwardes-Evans, Solicitor—legal consultant throughout.

Geoffrey Adams, Chief Executive, SIAD; Helen Auty, Assistant Secretary (Design), Royal Society of Arts; Leslie Julius, Director, Hille International Ltd; A.F.C. Miller (for Chapter 2).

Sections in Chapters 7 and 8: W.R.P. Adams, Director, British Carpet Manufacturers' Association; Christopher Attlee; Achillias Constantinou, Director, Ariella Fashions Ltd; Gordon Fairley, General Services Manager, Royal Yachting Association; P. Burns Farquar, Deputy Director General, British Jewellers' Association; Philip Fellows OBE DSC, lately Head of Exhibitions, Design Council; J.S. Forbes, Deputy Warden, Assay Office, Goldsmiths' Hall; Clifford Hatts, Head of Design Group, BBC TV; Arthur Katz CBE, Chairman, The Mettoy Company Ltd; Peter Lord, Austin-Smith:Lord; Julia Trevelyan Oman; Edward Pond; Ian Proctor; Richard Stevens, Head of Design, Post Office Telecommunications; Stuart Rose CBE.

Chapter 9: Françoise Jollant Kneebone, Centre de Creation Industrielle CCI, Paris; Claude Masouye, Director, Copyright and Public Information Department, World Intellectual Property Organisation; Richard Mayne, Commission of the European Communities, London.

Product illustrations: Ivan Engel, Managing Director, Den Permanente; Ron Hickman, Chairman, Tekron International Ltd; L.J. Thiselton, Patents Engineer, Hotpoint Ltd; H.D. Bickley, lately Head of Patents Branch, Post Office Telecommunications.

Secretarial work: Elizabeth Soulsbury; Graham and Pauline Thorn, The Cranbrook Stationery Co Ltd.

For the Design Council: Terry Bishop, Editor; Betty Dougherty, Graphic Design.

And, of course, Peter Kneebone for the illustrations.

Dan Johnston
1978

CHAPTER 1
Design and the Law

The introductory chapter to this book can be brief because so many writers and speakers on design in the past have felt it necessary to devote the first part of their book, article, speech or talk to arguing for the importance of design as a subject. This starting point now seems to be firmly established. It is also unnecessary here to trace the development of design through more than a century of industrial growth from its origins as an aspect of craftsmanship to its present position as an element in a country's economy. And during the past 20 years every possible design relationship seems to have been carefully studied – design and production, design and marketing, design and the consumer, the interest of Government, the education of the designer, the management of design, the growth of industrial design as a profession, and the distinctions between the roles of the industrial and the engineering designer.

For the purpose of this book it is sufficient to note that recognition had been given, even before the Industrial Revolution, to the need for the designer to be protected against those who would copy his work. It is necessary, however, to be clear about the arguments for design protection by law and also to restate the arguments against going too far.

There are two basic reasons why people become designers. The first depends on the fact that the job is an innovative and a creative one. This makes designing very satisfying to many intelligent people.

The second reason is, of course, that opportunities exist in design. Society needs creative people if progress is to be made. It needs them because change is inevitable in the modern world. The designer, the inventor and the entrepreneur, either as one person or as a team working together, are, in a material sense, the agents of change. They devise and then produce the new industrial products that become possible following scientific advance. They take account of social change, and from the nature of their work they also

7

help to bring it about. If one is an optimist one can believe that innovation and change bring the prospect of betterment – a higher standard of living, a better way of life for everyone.

There would seem then to be a good case for encouraging the innovator and protecting him by law against the plagiarist – the exploiter of the work of others. And there are supplementary reasons. The development of a marketable design from an original idea usually involves a great deal of expense in gradual modification as well as in final tooling up and laying down of appropriate plant. By no means all new, apparently good, ideas or designs succeed commercially. The entrepreneur is by definition a risk taker. If the copyist is to be permitted to move straight in at the production stage of the new but proven product, it is obvious that the innovator will be disillusioned or worse. Such a disincentive to producers of new designs must surely be a bar to progress.

Then again, the effectiveness of a country's industry is not only dependent on its productive efficiency; it is at least as dependent on whether or not it makes products that are in themselves desirable in the world's markets. This may turn on whether they make use of the most advanced technology, and also on whether or not they are up to date in the less tangible ways that make up the mix of a successful modern design. It may be argued, therefore, that the economic welfare of a country is bound up with ensuring a fair deal for the contributors of new, commercially practical ideas and designs.

There are, however, some counterbalancing points. It is obviously undesirable to give so much power to individuals, however talented they may be as inventors and/or designers, that they may be able to put a veto on the exploitation for the public good of the inventions or designs for which they have been responsible. Nor, leaving out the veto, should restriction due to patent law or design protection in whatever form be so considerable as to deprive the public of reasonable competition in the production of desirable products. A further point is that, in industries where fashion is a ruling factor, it is clearly undesirable to create a minefield of legal restrictions where a general sweep of changing taste is the periodic fact of life. Some people will always say that they sparked off such a change, but others will feel that they also contributed by intuitively sensing the way the winds of fashion were, in any case, blowing.

photograph Den Permanente

International 'trade'

The well-known Danish designer the late Kay Bojesen designed his wooden monkey in 1951. It was a great success. Some years later Den Permanente in Copenhagen put on a small display showing the Kay Bojesen monkey confronting its imitators (copies?) from the rest of the world. It is thought that the 'offspring' have all now died, but Den Permanente says that the original is still in good shape, several hundred being sold every year.

The outcome of these arguments is the generally accepted view that there should be encouragement for the innovator by giving him legal protection, provided that such protection does not unduly restrict the proper development of new products and the reasonable and fair exploitation of workable ideas. That this was the consensus view in 1962 is supported by the following statement from the Report of the Departmental Committee on Industrial Designs of that year chaired by Mr Kenneth Johnston QC:[1] 'The possibility that industrial designs ought not to have legal protection does not seem to be within our terms of reference ... Nevertheless, we think that we should record that our review of the subject leaves us in no doubt that legal protection for industrial designs should continue.' And the Report of the Committee to consider the Law on Copyright and Designs 1977, chaired by Mr Justice Whitford,[2] includes the sentence: 'It is our view that, in the industrial field as in other fields, the law should protect the proper interests of individuals creating works.'

9

Although the desire to give design protection seems to be well established, it cannot be argued that all has been, or is now, plain sailing. The law in Britain is undeniably complicated and there are some anomalies. This situation results from the nice balance of arguments about how much protection should be given, in what form and for how long. It must be coupled with the problem of keeping the law in step with rapid change in industrial and commercial society. The international situation, it may be added, is even more complicated because of variations in law and in practice between countries.

The outcome of all this is the fact that legal redress (and defence) seems to be unduly costly and slow, and the outcome is often difficult to predict. It may be that the same thing applies in other legal areas, but for many years there has been pressure in Britain and elsewhere to improve the law regarding design protection or to change it fundamentally. In Britain this led to the setting up of the two Departmental Committees referred to above.

Of the legal cases that are brought, the majority, as is to be expected, are settled out of court. Some trade associations, anxious to avoid legal costs for their members and at the same time to improve the design standing of their industry, set up panels of their own to arbitrate on suggestions of plagiarism between members. Also many manufacturers refuse to involve themselves in plagiarism issues, however good they think their case may be, saying that they count copying of their products as being the sincerest form of flattery.

Whether this is indeed the case, or whether legal remedies are too costly, too slow and too uncertain, or whether the manufacturer's own knowledge of the protection afforded by law is inadequate – these are the questions which it is hoped this book will answer.

WORDS AND PHRASES IMPORTANT
TO THE SUBJECT

This is a layman's book and for those who want authoritative sources there are references on pages 116 and 117. There are, however, some words or phrases that are important to the subject and which it may be useful to explain or define. This is done at the end of each of the early chapters.

INDUSTRIAL PROPERTY

The phrase has been in use for more than a century (Paris Convention for the Protection of Industrial Property 1883). It relates to those assets, some more tangible than others, of manufacturing or trading companies, which take the form of patents, registered designs, designs protected by copyright, together with associated know-how, and also to trade marks, and to trade and company names in respect of products produced and marketed by them.

INTELLECTUAL PROPERTY

The phrase is more recent. (It is referred to in the Whitford Report as 'today's jargon'.) There is, however, the World Intellectual Property Organisation (WIPO) with its head-quarters in Geneva. It was established in 1967 and became a 'specialised agency' of the United Nations in 1974. It has 73 Member States (see page 99).

The organisation says that:

'Intellectual property comprises two main branches:

industrial property, chiefly in inventions, trade marks and designs, and

copyright, chiefly in literary, musical, artistic, photographic and cinematographic works.

A substantial part of the activities and the resources of WIPO is devoted to assistance to developing countries. Particular emphasis is laid on the transfer of technology, including know-how, related to industrial property.'[3]

PLAGIARISM

A purloined idea, design, passage or work or the act or practice of plagiarising – the wrongful appropriation as one's own of the ideas or the expression of ideas of another.

COPY

A transcript or reproduction of an original work by someone else.

IMITATION

An artificial likeness, a thing made to look like something else which it is not.

INFRINGEMENT

The violation or breach of a code or law or statutory protection.

11

CHAPTER 2
Patent law

This book is about design protection and, in the main, the design envisaged is design for industry – design for commercial exploitation and for quantity production – rather than design for unique pieces or for very limited production by artists or by craftsmen. Protection by patent law is quite different from legal protection for designs, not only in Britain but internationally. That said, it may be fair to add that the differences in law and as seen by lawyers are greater than those seen by designers and manufacturers. A few designers are also inventors. All designers worthy of the name should at least be inventive and the distinction may sometimes seem to be slight. The new product of a designer and a manufacturer may possibly be best protected against copying by patenting it or by patenting an element in it. It may indeed be the only effective way of getting protection. For these reasons it is certainly necessary to have an early chapter in this book on patent law.

The history of patent law must be almost as old as the history of innovation related to the making of products in quantity. In a paper to the Royal Society of Arts,[4] Lord Nathan cited 'the earliest known patent for invention (or something like it)' as having been given by Henry VI in 1449 for the making of coloured glass for the windows of Eton College. And 'with the development of new industries in the reign of Elizabeth I patents became rather more common, about 50 being granted during her reign.'

In the Victorian period the pace of invention and industrial development led to much anxious thought and debate on patent law. The outcome was the Patent Act of 1852 on which the present British concepts of patent law are based. British law is now determined by the Patents Act 1977, which came into force in June 1978. The previous major Act was that of 1949 and its provisions are still important in respect of patents taken out under it. Now Britain is a member of the European Economic Community, much significance must be given to the Community Patent

Convention which is *not* yet in force ('Community Patents') and to the European Patent Convention which *is* in force. Patents under this latter Convention, which involves other European countries in addition to the nine, are granted by the European Patent Office with its headquarters in Munich. A major reason for the 1977 Act was the need to bring British law more closely into line with European thinking (see page 105).

Patent law *is* different from the law regarding design protection because patents relate to inventions, to workable new ideas. In turn these ideas (which are applicable to industry) will relate to products or processes; to machinery, to mechanisms, to electrical or electronic devices, to materials and their modification or synthesis, to chemical compositions and so on. Patents therefore are about ideas reduced to specific methods or processes of manufacture or to the workable product resulting.

Patents do *not* relate to design in the sense that design is the formulation of a product from an appearance point of view – the working out of a visual solution to an idea for a product.

A second big difference is that between the nature of the protection afforded by patent law and that by copyright. 'Patent law protects an invention by reserving for the owner of the patent the exclusive exploitation of the invention for a specified period. The protection of the invention is guaranteed by an act of state namely the grant of a patent.'[5] The patentee can prevent others from exploiting his invention. He has an exclusive right and the monopoly afforded by patent law is much broader than the protection afforded by design copyright – admittedly another exclusive right, but design copyright only gives the right to make copies of a particular design. (Design registration, however, as will be explained in detail in the next chapter, does give monopoly protection.)

Although the potential benefit to be derived from the grant of a patent may be very great indeed there are some drawbacks. To get a patent and then to maintain it is not cheap and can be very costly. There are many checks and queries to be coped with before the patent is granted. Even then the validity of the patent may still be challenged – in particular, by someone alleged to be infringing it.

The reason for the checks and balances is due, in large part, to the important element of public interest that applies so significantly to patent law. The granting of the patent to the individual for his prospective pecuniary benefit is counterbalanced by publication, not only of the nature of his invention, but also of how it can be made to work – how it can 'be performed by a person skilled in the art'.[7] The purpose of publication lies in the likelihood of benefit to the public. The alternative for the inventor of keeping his invention secret is seen as being damaging to the public interest in two ways. First, that the general body of scientific or technical knowledge will be the poorer, and second, that if the knowledge of the invention is not made public, there will be no way of ensuring that proper control is exercised over the way in which the patent is exploited.

The Patent Office is part of the Department of Trade and its function is to administer the Patents Act 1977 and its associated Rules (also the 1949 Act, and Rules, so far as their relevance continues). A British patent only gives protection in the United Kingdom.

The positive requirements laid down in the 1977 Patents Act for the grant of a patent are that the invention should be new; that it should involve an inventive step (be non-obvious); and that it should be capable of industrial application. The first piece of advice given by the Patent Office[6] is that an application for the grant of a patent must be accompanied by a specification and an abstract, both of which being specialised legal and technical documents, may best be drawn up by a patent agent. The value of a patent may be so great that there can be no doubt that this is sound advice. The Patent Office makes it clear that, while the grant of a patent gives the patentee the sole right to make, dispose of or use the invention during the period the patent remains in force, when the period expires, anybody else may then make use of the invention for which the patent was granted. The Patent Office warns that it does not give legal advice or opinions on any subject connected with patent law, and also, that it does not guarantee that the grant of a patent will enable the patentee to make any money from it!

It may be useful at this stage to explain the roles of the patent agent, the Patent Office Examiner and the lawyer – preferably a lawyer with special knowledge of patent law.

The patent agent has the particular skills and experience to enable him to write the best possible (most broadly drawn but still valid) specification from the applicant's point of view.

The Examiner is a civil servant and he must ensure that the specification is properly made out; that it adequately describes the invention (with the help of appropriate drawings in the prescribed form); that the invention is a real practical thing, not something theoretical – 'a discovery, a scientific theory or a mathematical method'[7] – or just an idea; and that there are proper instructions for making it work. He will carry out a search to establish whether it is indeed 'new', that 'it does not form part of the state of the art' – that it has not 'at any time before the priority date of that invention been made available to the public (whether in the United Kingdom or elsewhere) by written or oral description, by use or in any other way'; that the 'inventive step involved is not obvious to a person skilled in the art'; and that it 'can be made or used in any kind of industry, including agriculture'.[7] He will reject applications that are deemed to be frivolous – obviously contrary to well-established natural laws (such as perpetual motion machines) – as being incapable of industrial application. He will also exclude inventions 'the publication or exploitation of which would generally be expected to encourage offensive, immoral or anti-social behaviour' and 'any essentially biological process for the production of animals or plants, not being a micro-biological process or the product of such a process'.[7]

In the last resort, of course, the validity of a patent is determined not by the patent agent or the Examiner in the Patent Office, but in a court of law. There are provisions for application to be made by a third party for revocation of a patent but validity may also be challenged, and usually will be, when the owner of a patent claims that the patent has been infringed and the alleged infringer is brought to court.

PROCEDURE

1 The inventor (or joint inventors) or his (or their) employer, solely or jointly, make application to the Patent Office in London for a patent. This must (with rare exceptions) be done before the invention is publicly used or published. The application will normally, but not necessarily, be made through a patent agent and must be accompanied by a specification and an abstract.

The application may be a general statement, without

16

claims, that gives the applicant 12 months in which to file a further, more detailed application without losing priority. He can decide during this breathing space whether the invention is likely to justify the trouble and cost of proceeding further. Alternatively, the applicant may file his detailed application and claims immediately. The wording of the claims describing the invention is very important.

2 Preliminary examination and search. When a detailed application with claims is received it is referred to a Patent Office Examiner for a preliminary examination covering formal requirements and search. The results of this preliminary examination are communicated to the applicant. The application is given 'early' publication as soon as possible after 18 months from its priority date.

3 Substantive examination. If the applicant wishes to continue with his application (having considered the preliminary search report) he must make a request for substantive (technical) examination within six months of the date of publication of his application.

4 Grant of patent. If and when the application is found to be in order, the applicant is informed and notice of grant is advertised in the *Official Journal* (*Patents*) on payment of the appropriate fee.

5 Publication of the specification and other necessary detail is by its inclusion in the Patent Office Library and other libraries throughout the UK. An abstract of the specification, which must be supplied by the applicant when he makes his application, is also published by the Patent Office.

6 Revocation. At any time after the grant of a patent, any person may apply to the Comptroller of the Patent Office or to the courts to have the patent revoked – ie declared invalid on grounds specified in the Patents Act 1977.

7 Renewals. Action by the patentee is necessary. There is a special form which must be accompanied by the appropriate fee.

8 Assignments and Licences. The patentee may assign his patent or grant licences to use it and such arrangements should be registered at the Patent Office. Failure to do so can result in an assignee or exclusive licensee losing the right to claim damages for infringement occurring after the date of the assignment.

TIME TAKEN

The maximum time allowable by law is three and a half years from the priority date of the application – but it may take less. If the maximum period is exceeded the application is treated as withdrawn.

COST (at the time of writing)

Fees to the Patent Office

Up to the date of grant	£81 to £127
Before expiry of the fourth year from the date of patent and in respect of the fifth year	£40
Thereafter a fee is payable annually, the fee being at an increasing rate rising in the final year to	£108

Other fees will be payable for varied and additional procedures and to patent agents and lawyers if employed.

DURATION OF PROTECTION

Protection lasts for a maximum of 20 years from the date of filing the application. It lasts initially for a minimum of four years and thereafter may be extended up to the maximum on payment of the appropriate annual renewal fees.

(The 1977 Act increased the period from 16 to 20 years.) In certain cases extension may be possible but only where the patent was granted under the 1949 Act and where the applicant can show that he had not been able to benefit appropriately from the patent for reasons beyond his control.

MARKING

There is an advantage in the event of subsequent litigation in marking articles or the trade literature supporting them with the words 'Patent applied for' or 'Patent' with the number. Only the quoting of the number gives notice of the existence of the patent. If the number is omitted the patentee may find that he cannot claim damages.

CROWN RIGHTS

The Government reserves the right to use patented inventions 'for the services of the Crown'. In practice the right is mainly used in respect of the armed services and the Patent Office also has power to prohibit or restrict publicity when the defence of the realm or public safety could be endangered.

WORDS AND PHRASES IMPORTANT TO THE SUBJECT

NOVELTY

Novelty, in the sense of being new, different from anything before, is an essential requirement for the grant of a patent. The 1977 Act relates 'new' to 'the state of the art', 'whether in the United Kingdom *or elsewhere*'. To enable checks to be made as to what has gone before, the Patent Office maintains facilities for search.

INVENTIVE STEP

This is another essential requirement for a patent. A WIPO publication[3] says that a patentable invention 'must be non-obvious in the sense that it would not have occurred to any specialist in the particular industrial field, had such a specialist been asked to find a solution to the particular problem'. The 1977 Act says that: 'An invention shall be taken to involve an inventive step if it is not obvious to a person skilled in the art, having regard to any matter which forms part of the state of the art . . . '[7] at the time when the application was made.

SEARCH

In addition to the search undertaken by Patent Office Examiners, certain search facilities are also available to individual inventors and to patent agents. Search is through volumes of abridgements and abstracts of specifications which are indexed in great detail.

Examination and search are fundamental aspects of patent law in Britain. In some countries, before the 1977 Act became effective, the requirement for search was more extensive (but not necessarily more stringent) than here. In other countries patents are available simply on registration.

LICENCE OF RIGHT

The owner of a patent may apply to the Patent Office at any time after his patent has been granted for an entry to be made that licences are to be available as of right. The effects of such an entry are that renewal fees, from the time of the entry being made, are reduced by half and, on the other hand, if applicants for a licence cannot agree terms for a licence with the owner of the patent, the Comptroller of the Patent Office is empowered to determine the licence fee.

COMPULSORY LICENCES

It is in the public interest that patents, once granted, shall be used. It would be a negation of the whole purpose of patent law if a patentee could stifle benefit and progress by defending his patent and not using it himself.

Accordingly, if a UK patent has not been used (or not fully used), application may be made to the Comptroller for a licence to be granted or for an entry to be made making licences available, as of right. Such applications must be made on the grounds specified in the Act and must be justified by the applicant. One of the grounds for making such an application is that the terms proposed for a licence are so unreasonable as to unfairly prejudice 'the establishment or development of commercial or industrial activities in the United Kingdom'.[7] No such application may be made until three years after the patent has been granted.

PATENT OF ADDITION

Under the 1949 Patents Act modifications or additions could sometimes be made to an invention for which an application for a patent had been made or for which a patent had already been granted. There were special Patent Office arrangements for filing the new specifications but the 'patent of addition' would only run for the unexpired period of the original patent. 'Patents of addition' were of value if it was found in good time that the original specification was too narrow in its scope. Such patents are not admissible under the 1977 Act.

IMPROVEMENTS

When a patent is applied industrially it is quite possible, not only for a fund of manufacturing know-how to be built up, but also for significant new inventions to be made arising in some degree from the first.

When such inventions are patented they are sometimes

referred to as 'patents for improvement'. They date from the date of their filing and run for the full period. Such patents must be capable of standing up on their own. They give the patentee (usually the manufacturer) an important continuing advantage over competitors when the original patent expires.

CONVENTION COUNTRIES AND CONVENTION APPLICATIONS
The United Kingdom is a party to the Paris Convention for the Protection of Industrial Property. There are reciprocal rights between the Convention countries (and some other bilateral arrangements) whereby a person who has made application for a patent in a Convention country has the right, within twelve months from the date of the first application in a Convention country, to claim priority for an application in respect of the same invention in any other Convention country. Most of the industrialised countries of the world are parties to the Convention.

DESIGNING AROUND
If a manufacturer wants to use a patented invention he can approach the owner of the patent to negotiate a licence. Indeed, for many patentees the best way to exploit a patent is to license it to appropriate users. Subject to some limitations a patentee can make his own conditions and charge whatever he can get.

In competitive business the existence of an important patent in the hands of a competitor can be very serious. The competitor's patent and its potential may pose a threat to the whole future of a manufacturing business. And the competitor is quite likely to refuse a licence – or if he does make an offer the fee and/or conditions proposed may be thought to be unacceptable.

In such circumstances it is natural that an effort will be made to 'design around' – to find another mechanism, another device, another formula that will regain the prospect of future competitiveness which would otherwise seem to have been lost. It is obvious that a first step will often be to look again at earlier patents in the same field to see if a development based on one of them may perhaps avoid infringement of the competitor's patent. It may even be possible to cast doubt on the validity of his patent.

It should not be assumed that designing around is likely to provide an easy or an inexpensive alternative to licensing. It may, in fact, prove to be impossible.

21

Patents: a case history

WORKMATE: a folding, readily portable workbench/sawhorse incorporating a large, versatile vice. The unit is also useful as a mounting stand for power tools and generally for decorating.

Made by Black and Decker Ltd.

Invented and designed by Ron Hickman FSIAD. Developed in association with the Black and Decker design team.

1961–67	Basic idea gradually evolved by Ron Hickman into a practical product (WORKMATE Mark I).
1968	First four patents applied for in UK (granted 1972). Approaches made to major 'names' in the British tool and do-it-yourself industry (including Black and Decker) but rejected by all of them as not commercially viable.
	Mate Tools Ltd formed by the inventor to manufacture and market WORKMATE Mark I on a small but, as it turned out, impressively increasing scale.
1970–72	Development of Mark II design incorporating two working heights and other improvements. Further patents applied for in major countries throughout the world.
	Approaches by established manufacturers led to licensing terms being agreed for Black and Decker to manufacture and market WORKMATE throughout Europe.
Late 1972	Quantity production of Mark II. Marketed initially in UK but gradually extended throughout Europe.
1973	Design Council Award for WORKMATE Mark II. Licence agreed with Black and Decker to cover North America and all other parts of the world not covered by original European agreement.
	Steel increasingly used in construction instead of die-cast aluminium to ease production bottlenecks and keep cost down.
1974	New factory opened by Black and Decker at Kildare, Ireland, solely to produce WORKMATES (capacity 1

million units per annum). Manufacturing also in seven other countries.

1976   High Court action (UK) against alleged infringer. Mr Justice Graham said that for the purposes of his judgement it was not necessary to enlarge on recognition by the public of the value of the product. The defence had made it clear that the plaintiff 'in conceiving and marketing the WORKMATE had made a brilliant invention and done the public a great service'. Judgement in favour of patentee.

Low-cost, single-height designs added to the WORKMATE range.

1977   Court of Appeal (Lord Justice Buckley, Lord Justice Goff, Sir David Cairns). Patents again challenged on grounds of ambiguity of the claims, anticipation and obviousness of the invention. Judgement of the lower court upheld and found to be 'wholly unexceptional'. Leave to appeal to House of Lords refused.

The future

1989   Original UK patents expire. (They would have expired in 1985, but the 1977 Patents Act gave, in effect, a four-year extension.)

Beyond   Many other patents and design registrations covering the Mark II design, supplementary features and later designs will continue in force for several years more.

UNIT SALES

1968	Mark I	1,500 units
1977	principally Mark II	1·4 million units
1978	in all 13 variants	over2·0 million units projected

There are also 10 WORKMATE power tool accessories etc on sale in different parts of the world.

PATENTS, PATENT APPLICATIONS AND REGISTERED DESIGNS

Some 200 around the world (many of them in USA) and more to come. Cost so far some £250,000.

The trade mark WORKMATE is also protected by registration in all appropriate countries.

PATENT LITIGATION

Nineteen cases of alleged infringement throughout the world. Action successful or under way or settled out of court in UK, USA, West Germany, France and Japan. Cost so far some £300,000.

The WORKMATE story is, of course, a quite exceptionally successful one in commercial terms. It is equally remarkable, in an era of high technology, that the WORKMATE should be an essentially low-technology product—although this in no way underestimates the ingenuity that went into its invention. The invention has been backed up by strong patenting, determined litigation in support, continuous product development, and imagination and efficiency in production and marketing.

CHAPTER 3
Design registration

There is a surprisingly long history of legal protection for industrial designs in the UK (it goes back to 1787), and the protection until relatively recently was solely by monopoly rather than by copyright. As it is put in the Whitford Report,[2] 'protection for industrial designs was from the start, for no immediately apparent reason, on a monopoly basis (that is to say, protection against others marketing a substantially similar design whether or not actually copied).'

The registration of designs is the business of the Designs Registry, which has offices in London and Manchester. It is a branch of the Patent Office and the basis of its work is the Registered Designs Act 1949. The definition of 'design' in the Act, Section 1(3), is very important. It separates 'designs' from inventions and from patent law by emphasising appearance as distinct from constructional or functional qualities. 'Design' is said to mean 'features of shape, configuration, pattern or ornament applied to an article by an industrial process or means, being features which in the finished article appeal to and are judged solely by the eye, but does not include a method or principle of construction or features of shape or configuration which are dictated solely by the function which the article to be made in that shape or configuration has to perform.'

The official pamphlet on Protection of Industrial Designs[8] gives a shorter definition for design: 'the outward appearance of an article. Only the appearance given by its actual shape, configuration, pattern or ornament can be protected, not an underlying idea. "Article" also means any part of an article if that part is made and sold separately.'

The next chapter of this book is devoted to design protection by copyright, but something must be said first to put the Registered Designs Act of 1949 into proper perspective.

For many years prior to the Act there had been overlap between protection for designs by registration and automatic protection by copyright. The general trend of legislation and of supporting rules had been to reduce this overlap by giving copyright protection in this field only to artistic works and not to designs that were to be used industrially. The '50 rule' was introduced to withhold copyright protection from designs that were reproduced or 'intended to be reproduced in more than 50 single articles or made in lengths or pieces'. And the rules in support of the 1949 Act excluded from design registration:

'(1) Works of sculpture other than casts or models used or intended to be used as models or patterns to be multiplied by any industrial process

(2) Wall plaques and medals

(3) Printed matter primarily of a literary or artistic character, including bookjackets, calendars, certificates, coupons, dressmaking patterns, greetings cards, leaflets, maps, plans, postcards, stamps, trade advertisements, trade forms and cards, transfers and the like.'

Design registration is related to patent law because of the monopoly protection it affords. One difference, however, is that publication of the designs registered is more limited. The register of designs includes all the factual detail, but not an illustration of the design. The designs themselves are open to inspection, but, in respect of designs for wallpaper, lace and 'textile articles', only after two years (in some cases three years).

Searches are undertaken by staff of the Designs Registry when applications are made for designs to be registered. Also, 'if it is desired to know whether the design for an article is the same as, or closely resembles, any design registered in respect of the same kind of article and which is still a protected design, the Registry will conduct a search on application made ... accompanied by two representations or specimens of the design to be searched.'[8]

For a design to be registrable, the design must be 'new' at the date of application. It must not have been previously published, offered for sale or sold in the United Kingdom.

Design Registration under the 1949 Act, was, until 1968 when the Design Copyright Act became law, the only means of obtaining protection for a design for a product intended for quantity production. The number of designs registered averaged about 10,000 a year in the 1950s, but it had declined to less than half that number in 1975. The decline was very marked indeed in textile designs, which used to account for more than half of all designs registered, but are now down to less than 5 per cent of the annual total. Since 1968 registrations in areas other than textiles have remained fairly steady at some 4000 to 5000 a year. This is contrary to the general expectation that design registration would be virtually phased out with the passing into law of the Design Copyright Act.

The Johnston Committee (1962) recommended that design registration should be retained under the description of 'Design Monopoly'. It also recommended a new system of protection for designs to be known as 'Design Copyright' which would involve deposit of the design before publication but no search. This system was to run in parallel with 'Design Monopoly' but no legislative action was taken to give effect to these proposals.

The Whitford Committee (1977) recommended that 'registered design monopoly protection, as now provided by the Registered Designs Act 1949, should be repealed. Two members of the Committee however would not agree to such repeal unless the registration monopoly system were replaced by a design deposit system which would provide a valid priority basis for claims for protection overseas, under the Paris Industrial Property Convention.'[2]

For the present, design registration under the 1949 Act remains in force. Compared with protection by copyright, design registration has obvious disadvantages in terms of cost, the fact that a certain amount of time is taken to achieve protection, the difficulties arising from the requirement for novelty and the practical problems of search. Also the words in the Act 'features of shape, configuration' etc, give a more limited definition for protection by design registration than is the case with design copyright. On the other hand there are some quite tangible advantages to be derived from a system of design registration. It is known that the registered design has satisfied some sort of test, that the designer or manufacturer has taken trouble and paid money to have it registered – in effect, competitors have been warned that the design is a valued one. The registration gives the owner of the design a basis from which he can defend his property. Finally, the nature of monopoly protection *is* more broadly based than protection by copyright.

PROCEDURE

1 The designer (or more usually the firm he works for or the firm to which he has sold the design) or someone importing a design, applies to the Designs Registry in London (or Manchester for textiles) for registration of the design. The application will normally, but not necessarily, be made through a patent agent, most of whom also deal with design registration.

2 Submission of the application form. There are six types of form, some of them specifically relating to textiles. The application must be accompanied by representations or specimens of the design and, except in the case of textiles or wallpaper, a statement of the features of the design 'for which novelty is claimed, ie whether for shape or configuration or pattern or ornament or for a combination of any of these four features'.[8]

3 Examination and search (not for some items of textiles) is made by staff of the Designs Registry. If no objection follows, the design will then be registered and a Certificate of Registration will be issued. The validity of a registration may, of course, be challenged by anyone accused by the proprietor of a registered design of producing a design thought to be too similar to it.

4 Renewals. Action is necessary by the owner of the registered design. There are special forms which must be accompanied by the appropriate fee.

5 Assignments and Licences. The owner of a registered design may assign or grant licences to use his design and such arrangements are required to be registered at the Designs Registry.

TIME TAKEN

The maximum allowable by law is 15 months from the date of application to completion of the registration. Without special application the maximum is 12 months and frequently the time taken will be appreciably less, perhaps only two or three months.

COST (at the time of writing)

Fees to the Designs Registry (payable to the Patent Office)
On application £5 to £42
Extension for a second
period of five years £52
Extension for a third
period of five years £74

Other fees will be payable for varied and additional procedures and to patent agents and lawyers if employed.

DURATION OF PROTECTION

Protection lasts initially for five years from the date of application for registration. With the two further periods of five years, protection is for a maximum of 15 years.

MARKING

It is not a requirement that registered designs when marketed should be marked to indicate their registration. There is, however, a potential advantage in marking should there be subsequent litigation. It is advisable to mark with the registration number as well as the words 'registered design'. If the number is omitted the owner of the registered design may find that he cannot claim damages.

CROWN RIGHTS

The Government reserves the right, as with patents, to use registered designs for the services of the Crown, but this rarely arises.

WORDS OR PHRASES IMPORTANT TO THE SUBJECT

NEW AND/OR ORIGINAL

These words frequently occur in copyright and design protection legislation. The official pamphlet[8] gives two aspects of meaning for the requirement that a design must be new at the date of application for its registration: first, it must not have already been published – offered for sale or sold by the applicant; second, it can be said to be new 'if, when compared with any other published design for the same or any other type of article, the differences in shape, configuration, pattern or ornament (but excluding any difference of a kind commonly used in the trade as a variation) make a materially different appeal to the eye when each article is viewed as a whole'. 'Original' in copyright law means quite simply 'originating from the author as his own work'.[1] Some authorities also see the word 'original' as used in design law, as providing an alternative to 'new' by making registration of a design possible, if the design itself is not new, but has been applied to a new sort of article or applied in a new way.

TRADE VARIANT

'Variants commonly used in the trade' are not registrable under the Registered Designs Act 1949. The principle is that the 'newness' required for registration involves more in skill, labour and original thought than the routine manipulation of well-established design elements.

FAIR FOLLOWER

The report of the Johnston Committee[1] explains that this term is used to describe a design 'which is the same in general style and idea as a protected design, but which differs in detail to such a degree that it cannot be said that it reproduces the design to a substantial extent. In other words, fair followers copy, indeed they represent, the trend. We [the Johnston Committee] are in full agreement with the view that the making of fair followers is a permissible activity.'

It must be emphasised that the law protects designs – not the ideas behind them. In this respect there is a major difference between the law of design protection and patent law, where the aim is to offer protection to the originators of ideas which can be made to work.

CONVENTION COUNTRIES AND CONVENTION APPLICATIONS

The Registered Designs Act 1949 gives force to the terms of the Paris Convention for the Protection of Industrial Property to which the United Kingdom is a party. 'A person who has made application for the protection of a design in a Convention country has the right, within six months from the date of the first application in a Convention country, to claim priority of that date in an application in respect of the same design in any other Convention country.'[8]

Most of the industrialised countries of the world are parties to the Convention.

CHAPTER 4
Design copyright

The first Copyright Act in British law dates back to Queen Anne and the year 1709. The development of copyright law since then has run parallel with the development of patent law – the one concerned with encouragement and protection for the inventor and his workable ideas, the other with encouragement and protection for the creative worker and the works on which he exercises his labour and skill. As the Whitford Report[2] says, 'Copyright protection finds its justification in fair play. A person works and produces something. The product of his skill and labour ought to belong to him (or possibly to his employer) . . . A writer writes an article about (for example) the baking of bread. He puts words on paper. He is not entitled to a monopoly in the writing of articles about the baking of bread, but the law has long recognised that he has an interest not merely in the manuscript, the words on paper which he produces, but in the skill and labour involved in his choice of words and the exact way in which he expresses his ideas by the words he chooses.'

Copyright protection has been gradually extended from articles and books to other forms of literature, to music, to works of art and architecture, to 'works of artistic craftsmanship', and to many less obvious products of creative labour and skill such as mathematical tables, price lists, advertising material and football pool coupons. The law is based at present on the Copyright Act 1956. Literary, dramatic, musical and 'artistic works' are covered in Part I; sound recordings, films, television and sound broadcasts come in Part II.

Protection by copyright is protection for original work against the act of copying. Ideas are not protected. Protection is for the works themselves – the piece of writing, the piece of music, the particular painting, sculpture, drawing or photograph – and many other 'works'.

It may be true that someone, by coincidence and quite independently, has produced a work that is virtually the same as one by another person. This sort of thing happens

D.P.– C

33

and neither person need be a copyist. One of the two may have preceded the other in publishing his work, but that in itself will not be conclusive proof that the second person to publish has copied the first. In such a case the author of the first work cannot prevent the author of the second one from publishing his equally original work. Both have copyright and can prevent others from copying. If the same thing happened in respect of inventions, the first of which had been patented, or designs, the first of which had been registered, monopoly protection would be available to the proprietor of the patent or the registered design. There is the possibility, of course, that the validity of the patent or registered design might be challenged and would have to be sustained in any legal action taken against the alleged infringer.

Although copyright protection is more limited than that given by patent law or by design registration, protection by copyright is automatic and immediate. There are no fees to pay, no forms to fill in, and no patent agents to employ. Copyright applies at once and without fuss to original works, whether published or unpublished. The term of protection is in general for the life of the author of the work plus 50 years from his death or 50 years from the date of publication of the work, whichever is the later.

Reference has already been made to the overlap between the law of copyright and the law concerning design protection prior to the Registered Designs Act of 1949. In the words of the Whitford Report, the Copyright Act of 1956 gave 'copyright protection to designs through the provision for drawings and to some extent also through the provisions for "works of artistic craftsmanship" '.[2] Drawings were seen as constituting the 'artistic work' and they were very broadly defined in the Act to include 'any diagram, map, chart or plan' and subsequently engineering drawings were also deemed to be included by Court ruling. By the provisions of the Act it was further established that copyright in a drawing could 'be infringed by making an object in three dimensions, provided that non-experts' could 'see that the three-dimensional object' was 'a reproduction of the two-dimensional artistic work and because it did not require an expert to identify the relationship'.[9] As explained in the previous chapter (page 26), some important groups of artistic or design works were excluded from registration under the Registered Designs Act. Such designs continued to have copyright protection after the 1956 Act, but copyright was withdrawn if a design was registered or 'applied industrially' (reproduced in more than 50 articles).

In 1962 the Johnston Committee recommended the introduction of a system of design copyright that would have involved the deposit of specimens of the design to be protected, with payment of the appropriate fee but no search. The designs deposited were to have been open to public inspection. Although the recommendations of the Johnston Committee were much praised and there was considerable agitation to get legislative action, none was forthcoming. The reason was said to be that a major piece of legislation would be necessary and parliamentary time was not available.

Instead, in 1968, a little-noticed private member's Bill was passed into law as the 1968 Design Copyright Act. It was introduced by Mrs Jill Knight MP and sponsored in the House of Lords by Lord Cawley. It had Government support and was not opposed.

Announcing the change, the then Board of Trade explained that under the Copyright Act 1956 a design in the form of a drawing had initial protection 'irrespective of artistic quality', subject to some provisos. The design must have had sufficient skill and labour expended on it to make it an 'artistic work' and it must be original in the sense that it was the designer's own work and not a copy of someone else's. The protection meant that the design might not be copied either in two or three dimensions. The new Act would give copyright protection for 15 years to products produced industrially and based on such drawings. (As already mentioned, there was the parallel possibility of protection for designs, also produced industrially, and originating as 'works of artistic craftsmanship'.) Protection by design registration would continue; the Design Copyright Act would provide an 'additional remedy'.[10]

It was further explained that, although the new Act did not accord in detail with the recommendations of the Johnston Committee, it would be simpler to operate and there was no reason why it should not work satisfactorily to meet the needs of those industries for which design registration was unsatisfactory. It was also felt that the protection given would be in a fairer form. Another point made was that the enactment of the new law would 'automatically provide a measure of protection for United Kingdom designs in a number of European countries, under the Berne Copyright Convention, without any need to register in those countries'.[10]

The Whitford Report[2] says that 'the wide implications of the 1968 Design Copyright Act were not appreciated immediately in industry' and notes later that the Act had 'effectively gone a lot further than the Johnston recommendations of 1962'. It also refers to the 'very rough and ready manner' in which provision for copyright protection was made 'over a very wide field but only if the design happens to have originated as a drawing'.

It is certainly the case that two or three years went by before designers or industrialists realised that the Act had given greatly increased prospects for effective defence against copyists. It is equally true that the 1968 Act (together with court rulings) has produced some anomalous situations and unexpected difficulties. In part these led to the setting up of the Whitford Committee in 1974.

One anomaly arises from the preferential position for designs that are capable of copyright protection, but would not be registrable. Such designs, which are unregistrable because they are too dependent on functional requirements or because they fall into the categories that are specifically excluded in the 1949 Registered Designs Act, have been held to be eligible for the full 'life plus 50 years' copyright protection.[11] [12]

Another anomaly, intrinsic in the 1968 Act, is that copyright of an industrial product is utterly dependent on protection for the drawings or possibly the 'work of artistic craftsmanship' on which the design of the product is based. However, many designers of three-dimensional products prefer to work in three dimensions from the beginning, and there may not be any drawings. The models they make may be adequate for their purpose, but they may not be in the ordinary sense 'artistic' or even particularly good as examples of 'craftsmanship'. The courts have also found it difficult to accept that a work is a 'work of artistic craftsmanship' if it has a functional basis.[13] The biggest industrial problem to arise has been with businesses producing spare parts for motor vehicles. Copying of the design of parts for sale as spares had been an accepted fact of life in the car industry. With changes in the industry and then the passing into law of the 1968 Act, what had been established practice became a matter for legal actions or the threat of them.

Since the 1968 Design Copyright Act made such an important change in the law concerned with design protection it is important to consider the matter of retrospection.

There are two important dates: the date when the 1956 Copyright Act came into force, which is June 1957; and the comparable date for the 1968 Act, which is October 1968. If the drawings for the design were done after June 1957 a claim to copyright can be based on them. If they were done before that date it is less certain. As regards the second date, October 1968, copies of industrially made products, not of registered design but based on drawings of valid copyright, made before that date will not be an infringement. Identical products made after that date will infringe.

There is the usual uncertainty if the claim to copyright is based on 'works of artistic craftsmanship', but the same principles apply as to dates.

THE WHITFORD REPORT: RECOMMENDATIONS

The Whitford Committee was divided, sometimes three ways, over improvement in the law of design copyright. Perhaps the most controversial of the Committee's proposals was that there should be two categories of designs – category A and category B. Category A would include 'designs consisting only of surface pattern and the shapes of three-dimensional articles of which the aesthetic appearance will influence a purchaser in making a purchase'. Category B would include 'all shapes of three-dimensional articles where the appearance of the article does not influence the purchaser, who buys the article only in the expectation that it will do the job for which it is intended'.

In respect of designs in category A, the members were agreed about the desirability for the continuation of design copyright protection and recommended a 25-year term to conform with the latest text of the Berne Convention. As to category B, the members were divided three ways as to whether and in what form protection should be afforded by copyright.

There are suggestions in the report for the removal of acknowledged anomalies and a system of compulsory licensing is recommended for designs of a functional character 'where the United Kingdom market is not being adequately supplied by manufacturers within the (European) Community'. (The Summary of Recommendations of the Whitford Committee is given as an Appendix to this book on page 113.)

PROCEDURE

The only action the designer or the manufacturer need take is to record the date of first publishing (marketing) the design. Copyright is automatic and immediate. There are no formalities and there is no cost (see also pages 70 and 80).

ASSIGNMENTS AND LICENCES

The owner of a copyright is the 'author of the work' – the designer – but where he is employed by someone else the copyright belongs to the employer. The copyright in a work may be transferred to others or a licence or licences may be arranged. It is important to get all such arrangements into good legal form.

DURATION OF PROTECTION

Design copyright extends for 15 years from the date of first marketing the product.

MARKING

It is not necessary in British law for works on which copyright is claimed to be marked ©, but it is a requirement in some other countries with which Britain has arrangements for reciprocal copyright protection. If the work on which copyright is claimed has relevance in these other countries, the mark must be applied, together with the copyright owner's name and the year of publication. If the work is a product to which the mark cannot be applied, then the mark should be made on the packaging or on any related brochures or other explanatory literature. The supporting commercial literature should itself be indicated as being protected by copyright.

For the future, about industrial designs (and in particular the proposed category A), the Whitford Report[2] says: 'To ensure adequate notice of the claim to protection (by copyright) damages should not be recoverable in respect of infringement committed before specific notice of the claim to copyright or unless notice has been given by way of marking . . .'

CROWN COPYRIGHT

The copyright of works commissioned by or produced under the direction of government departments belongs to the Crown, but is not always enforced.

WORDS OR PHRASES IMPORTANT TO THE SUBJECT

CORRESPONDING DESIGN
In the words of the 1956 Act, 'corresponding design', in relation to an artistic work, means a design which, when applied to an article, results in a reproduction of that work. In layman's terms it means the actual product produced and marketed based on the drawings or 'work of artistic craftsmanship' that have copyright protection.

BERNE COPYRIGHT CONVENTION
The United Kingdom has ratified the 1948 Brussels text of the Berne Convention for the Protection of Literary and Artistic Works but not the 1971 Paris text. There are relatively few important countries that are not covered by the Berne Convention or by other treaties (the USSR and China are exceptions). The USA is not a signatory of the Berne Convention, but is a member country of the Universal Copyright Convention (see below). The general rule is that countries accord the same copyright protection to works from nationals of other member countries as they do to their own nationals. One of the recommendations of the Whitford Report[2] is that the operation of this principle should be tightened up so that 'foreigners should not get more automatic protection here than they give us in their respective countries' (see also page 104).

UNIVERSAL COPYRIGHT CONVENTION (UCC)
This convention dates from 1952 and the latest text revision, in 1971, has been ratified by the UK.

The Convention provides for 'a minimum period of copyright protection of ten years for photographs and works of applied art if protected as such'. It limits the formalities which any country may demand to use of 'the symbol © with the year date of first publication and the name of the copyright owner'[2] (see also page 105).

CHAPTER 5
Trade marks, brand names and company symbols

The World Intellectual Property Organisation defines a trade mark as 'a sign which serves to distinguish the goods (as does the "service mark" with regard to services) of an industrial or a commercial enterprise or a group of such enterprises'.[3] Trade marks have been important in national and international business for very many years.

British law concerning trade marks is dependent on the Trade Marks Act 1938 and the Trade Marks Rules of the same year, with subsequent amendments. However, legal protection for trade marks goes back very much further than that. Also, legal remedies are provided in other ways against misleading business practices. This aspect of the law, which is relevant to design protection, is known as the law concerning 'passing off'. It will be dealt with in the next chapter.

The office of the Registrar of Trade Marks is at the Patent Office, which therefore deals with trade mark registration as well as with patents and design registration. One of its official pamphlets[14] says that a trade mark is 'a means of identification . . .a symbol (whether word, device or a combination of the two) which a person uses in the course of trade in order that his goods may be readily distinguished by the purchasing public from similar goods of other traders'. In another definition,[15] a mark, to be registrable as a trade mark, must 'indicate a connection in the course of trade between the owner of the mark and his goods. It does not matter what sort of trade connection; manufacturers, dealers, importers, even people who never own the goods, can all have trade marks.'

The use of the word 'symbol' in the Patent Office definition raises an immediate question as to the distinction, if any, between a trade mark and a company symbol. The answer is that many company symbols are also registered as trade marks and, as such, are seen by their proprietors as valuable items of industrial property. They constitute one of the most tangible aspects of company goodwill.

41

'BP in shield' is registered as a trade mark in the UK and in many other countries. It is perhaps the best known British mark in the world and although the registration of marks so clearly dependent on two initial letters is exceptional, its registration has been justified by its extensive use in respect of a wide range of goods.

This trade mark is registered in the UK and very widely used throughout the world. Formica International Limited has always taken every precaution against misuse of the word 'FORMICA' and takes very strong action against offenders. 'FORMICA' is an invented word and must only be used for products of the Formica Group of Companies, either all in capitals or with a capital 'F', never with a small 'f', and as an adjective—for example FORMICA plastic laminate—never as a noun.

Marks and Spencer's trade mark is registered world-wide in respect of the goods marketed by the company. The mark was challenged some years ago in France by a trade mark plagiarist claiming non-usage by Marks and Spencer in that country. Marks and Spencer say 'not only had we, in fact, exported clothing under our mark: the infringing mark was also ordered by the French court to be expunged in all classes, including those in which we had not yet traded but intended to trade, on the grounds of the fraudulent intent in registering the mark'.

The CAMRA logo (in the shape of a beer mug) is registered as a trade mark in respect of publications, clothing and glassware. There has been no attempt to register the logo for beer itself because, as the organisation says, 'we are not in business selling or brewing beer ourselves'. The actual word CAMRA and the organisation's full name (Campaign for Real Ale Ltd) are not, however, registered as trade marks.

Many other company and other organisation symbols are not registered as trade marks, either through simple failure to register them or because, for very good reasons, they are not eligible for registration. That is not to say that company symbols, as part of corporate identity programmes, are not valuable. Trade marks, quite clearly, have an immediate commercial purpose; the value of corporate identity programmes (and of the symbols that are usually an element in them) is more general. Certainly commercial considerations come into it, but they may be long-term ones. The immediate gain may be in giving a sense of unity to a group of recently merged companies; a boost in morale to a company's workpeople by giving them an acceptable and frequent visual reminder of the firm's various activities; or help in bringing the organisation to wider and more favourable public attention.

Returning to the requirements for registration of trade marks, and taking positive things first, in order to be registrable, a trade mark must be distinctive. It must be distinctive in association with the products to which it relates – a mark that is memorable. The 1938 Act says that if a trade mark is to be registered, 'it must contain or consist of at least one of the following essential particulars:

(a) the name of a company, individual, or firm represented in a special or particular manner
(b) the signature of the applicant for registration or some predecessor in his business
(c) an invented word or invented words
(d) a word or words having no direct reference to the character or quality of the goods, and not being according to its ordinary significance a geographical name or a surname
(e) any other distinctive mark . . .'

In addition to the insistence on distinctiveness, the other big positive requirement in British law is that 'registration of trade marks is limited to marks used or proposed to be used in relation to goods'[14] – to specific classes of materials or products of which 34 are listed (some in considerable detail). These range from chemical products through machines and machine tools, building materials, furniture, mirrors and picture frames, clothing including boots, shoes and slippers, tobacco, raw and manufactured, smokers' articles and matches. Registration for trade marks does not apply 'to goods in general . . . Each application for registration must specify the particular goods in respect of which registration is sought.'[14]

This requirement implies the first of the negative points and explains why many well-known symbols are not registrable as trade marks. 'There is no provision for the registration of trade marks used for services eg garages, laundries etc.' This means that some well-known symbols such as that for British Rail are not registered.

Of the other negatives, many are very much to be expected. Brand names are quite possible (as invented words) but it must be remembered that words 'appeal to the ear as well as to the eye'. It is reasonable therefore that 'phonetic renderings of known words' or words 'grotesquely mis-spelt', as one judge aptly put it, will be refused. As the words in the Act imply, it will be difficult to register 'surnames, geographical names, mere letters and numerals' and to justify 'words which refer directly to the characteristics of the goods', words that are reminiscent of the material from which the product is made or which imply excellence in some way. Trade mark registration will be refused for any mark that is 'contrary to law or morality' or for 'any scandalous design'. Representations of the Queen or members of the Royal Family or inclusion of the Royal arms, crests and the like are not allowed, nor are the national flags of Britain and other countries. Similarly, certain devices associated with the armed forces are ruled out and so are words such as 'Royal', 'Imperial' and 'Anzac', which may be 'likely to lead persons to think that the applicant either has or recently has had Royal patronage or Government authorisation'. Applications may also be refused where words such as 'patent', 'patented', 'registered' or 'Red Cross' are included or where there are representations of crosses in red on white or the reverse or similar. More generally, 'it would not be right to allow the registration of trade marks which are identical or confusable with words or symbols (whether or not used as trade marks) which other traders in the goods should be free to use in the ordinary course of business'. Any further registration will not be agreed for proposed trade marks that are 'identical with or nearly resemble other trade marks already registered in the name of other proprietors in respect of the same or similar goods'. (There is provision for exceptional consideration 'in the case of honest concurrent use or of other special circumstances'.)

Finally there is a very important requirement, which is

The British Rail symbol is not registered (and is not registrable) as a trade mark in the UK because it is used in relation to services rather than goods. It is, however, registered in France because the French system caters for 'service marks' and British Rail ships sail as part of Sealink ferry services.

The Royal Society for the Protection of Birds has not felt it necessary to register its symbol as a trade mark, and although the symbol has been in use since 1969, there has been no trouble with infringements. The mark probably could be registered because the Society has a considerable range of literature that carries the mark, and it also markets giftware. The RSPB is, however, a charity and it might be argued that the money could be better spent.

The provision of car parking facilities is clearly a service, so no attempt has been made to register the National Car Parks Ltd symbol. NCP found from a survey that it is one of the best known symbols in the UK. The company does not mind if other organisations use similar signs because it simply means more publicity for NCP.

The Royal Shakespeare Company's symbol was redesigned in 1977. The swan emblem and the initials RSC were combined in such a way that many variants could be produced to cover the numerous activities of the company. There has been no attempt to register the mark. The main theatrical business of the company can certainly not be described as trade in goods (though registration could nevertheless perhaps be achieved in respect of the company's printed matter). However, the RSC no doubt feels that plagiarism of its symbol is unlikely—and if it happened, it would not be too difficult to overcome.

fundamental to trade mark law. This is that a trade mark must not be misleading to the public or deceptive in any way 'eg in suggesting, even if not directly stating, that the goods concerned possess characteristics which they do not'.

Most trade mark registration is handled by the trade mark agents or by patent agents, most of whom also undertake trade mark work. The Trade Marks Registry of the Patent Office receives applications for registration, but there is another office in Manchester (dealing with marks for textile goods) and in Sheffield there is a special case: trade mark applications for 'metal goods' by persons 'carrying on business in Hallamshire or within six miles thereof' may be made to the Cutlers' Company. As with patents, there are facilities for anyone to search, on payment of a fee, through classified indexes of trade marks already registered. Search may also be made through other marks for which application has been made. Trade marks are normally registered irrespective of colour; if there is a colour limitation there will be a note on the registration to that effect.

Trade marks are registered in Part A or Part B of the Register and give monopoly protection against others using or seeking to use the same or similar marks in the classes of goods specified in the registration. Registration in Part A calls for a better demonstration that the requirement for 'distinctiveness' has been met than does registration in Part B. There is no requirement that trade marks shall or shall not have had prior use by the proprietor before application for registration is made. It is obviously unwise to neglect, or intentionally to defer, application for registration of a trade mark because someone else with a similar mark may come along and pre-empt the application. However, association of a mark in the public's mind with particular goods does help to establish 'distinctiveness'. Indeed application may, and usually should, be made to transfer trade marks registered in Part B to the more valuable Part A after use has helped to build up goodwill associated with the mark. The owner of a Part B mark, as compared with a Part A, has less protection against others using a trade mark similar to his if the other party can prove that there was no intention to mislead.

The value of trade marks, whether registered or not, and whether in Part A or Part B, lies in their recognition value in respect of products – new products or established ones. A well-known trade mark with a product of proven worth gives the consumer an easily recognisable reminder of past satisfaction. With a new product the known trade mark gives an implied recommendation to potential users as soon as the product is marketed. Product goodwill can thus be built up and existing company goodwill can be enhanced through intelligent use of trade marks. Registration gives immediate protection for the trade mark against possible infringers and if there is litigation it will be easier to get redress than by relying on a claim for 'passing off'. Another quite tangible advantage of registration is that a mark that has been registered cannot be held to infringe another more recently established mark even if that mark is also accepted for registration. It is never safe for a trader to illustrate another company's trade mark in promotional or even informative literature, however careful the wording.

Trade marks are often licensed by their owners for use by other firms with which they have a business connection. The subject is a difficult one since the provisions of British law are not general. Good legal advice about such licensing is essential (see page 53).

A high proportion of the trade marks registered are word marks (words or groups of words which can be printed in any typeface). The alternative is a device mark and to design such a trade mark is a test of skill for the most able of designers.

New device marks should not only be up to date in their graphic design treatment; they must be able to stand the test of time and changing taste. A mark that is readily acceptable to the intended proprietor may be so because it fits a design style that is well established and may even be becoming dated. Before long such a trade mark will have acquired a character that will be an embarrassment to the firm, and especially to its marketing people.

Minor changes are possible to keep an established mark in line with changes in design thinking, but such changes call for good design advice and careful consideration by lawyers and/or trade mark agents. The registration of a new mark to replace an old one will risk the loss of important goodwill. There will also, of course, be new costs which can be very considerable if the mark has to be registered in many other countries as well as the UK.

The Mathys Committee[16] was set up in 1972 to report on the state of British law concerning trade marks. Its report was presented to Parliament in 1974. The Committee

Certification trade marks

The Kitemark is a registered certification trade mark owned by British Standards Institution. The mark was first registered in 1904 and is probably the earliest known certification trade mark. The mark is granted to manufacturers who are capable of manufacturing a product to the requirement of a British Standard and they are inspected by BSI Inspectorate who in addition remove samples of the product for independent testing. The Kitemark is the recognition by BSI that a product is being manufactured to the requirements of a British Standard.

The Harris Tweed mark is registered in the UK and 26 other countries. The words are not an integral part of the registered mark, but the definition which was accepted by a Scottish court says that 'Harris Tweed means a tweed made from pure virgin wool produced in Scotland, spun, dyed and finished in the Outer Hebrides and hand-woven by the islanders at their own homes in the islands of Lewis, Harris, Uist, Barra and their several purtenances and all known as the Outer Hebrides'. The Harris Tweed Association Ltd owns the mark, polices the rules and defends it as necessary.

The Woolmark is second in usage in Britain to the BSI Kitemark. It is widely registered throughout the world. The prime purpose of the mark is to ensure that products made from wool are properly identified and the mark is also a guarantee against adulteration with other fibres. As with all certification trade marks, there are precise rules for the use of the Woolmark. There can be good reasons for blending wool with other fibres, so there is also a Woolblendmark which is operated in a similar way.

real leather

The Leathermark is the property of The Leather Institute and is used extensively in the UK, France, Italy and Germany. It is not registered as yet, but an application has been made for registration as a certification trade mark, which takes a considerable time. The mark signifies 'real leather' as defined in a British Standard. A licensing scheme is being worked out with different forms of wording to indicate which parts of an article the mark refers to and what type of leather is used. There have been no problems with imitators or with misuse.

recommended that the UK 'should continue to support international treaties aimed at assisting international trade by simplifying procedures for the registration and protection of trade marks'. The UK should 'continue to co-operate in the negotiations for the proposed convention for a European trade mark' (see page 106). 'Due attention should (also) be paid to the developments in the EEC relative to trade mark law and practice, in particular the practical, as well as legal, results of a transition from nine nationally protected markets to a common market . . .'[16]

Specific changes proposed for British law included provision for the registration of 'service marks' – 'marks used or proposed to be used for distinguishing services offered in the course of trade or business' and it was also recommended that 'Part A and B of the register should be merged'.[16]

Legislation has not as yet been introduced to give effect to these recommendations.

PROCEDURE

1   The Proprietor of a trade mark used or proposed to be used in the UK applies to the Trade Marks Registry at the Patent Office in London (or if appropriate in Manchester or Sheffield) for registration of the mark. The application must be in the name of the user or the intended user – not the designer – otherwise registration may be invalid. The application will normally, but not necessarily, be made through a trade mark agent or a patent agent.

   Preliminary advice may be obtained from the Trade Marks Registry, on payment of a fee, as to the distinctiveness of a proposed mark and a request may be made for search in respect of possible conflicting marks, before application is made for registration.

2   Submission of the application form. The form (a special one for textiles) must be accompanied by representations of the mark, mounted in the required way, and a separate application must be made 'for goods in each class in which the mark is to be registered'. The experience of the trade mark or patent agent is of great value in achieving the widest possible description of the goods to which it is intended that the mark will be applied.

3   Examination and search is made by staff of the Trade Marks Registry. If the trade mark for which application

for registration has been made complies with the provisions of the Act and Rules; if the mark is distinctive, not deceptive, and does not 'conflict with other marks already registered or currently applied for in respect of the same type of goods', then—

4 Acceptance by the Registrar is notified.

5 Advertisement is then made of a representation of the mark and details relating to it in the *Trade Marks Journal.*

6 Opposition may be made by interested parties within laid down time limits. An objection made at this stage has more chance of succeeding than at any time later.

7 If there is no opposition, or the opposition fails, a Certificate of Registration is issued.

8 Renewals. Action by the trade mark proprietor is necessary. There is a special form which must be accompanied by the appropriate fee.

9 Assignments (with or without goodwill). The new proprietor is required to register his title with the Trade Marks Registry. There may be legal difficulties about proof of title if this is not done and there are powers to preclude the transfer of trade marks where the result would be to confuse or mislead.

10 Licences – Registered users. The use of a registered trade mark by someone other than the registered proprietor should be registered and the Registrar must approve the details 'as not being contrary to the public interest'.

He may lay down 'suitable conditions or restrictions where necessary', particularly in relation to the standard and quality of the goods upon which the trade mark is to be used.

The principle once again is that the public shall not be misled so 'there must be a connection in the course of trade between the registered user and the goods on which he exercises his "permitted use" of the mark'.[14]

TIME TAKEN

So far as the applicant is concerned the work of registration of a trade mark is required to be completed in 12 months, but it may take less and frequently, at the discretion of the Registrar, further time will be allowed.

COST (at the time of writing)

Fees to the Trade Mark Registry (actually payable to the Patent Office) are:

On application	£20
On registration	£30

Renewals (see under 'duration of protection' below) £73 Other fees will be payable for varied and additional procedures and to trade mark or patent agents or to lawyers if employed.

DURATION OF PROTECTION

Initially for seven years and then renewable for periods of 14 years. If a trade mark is not used for five years and the owner cannot show very good 'special circumstances' beyond his control that prevented its use, the right to the registration may be lost. After the initial period of seven years it is very unlikely that the validity of a Part A trade mark can be successfully challenged.

MARKING

There is no requirement in the UK for registered trade marks to carry any indication that they have been registered. It is frequent practice, however, to indicate registration by the words 'registered trade mark'. In the USA there is optional marking and one of the marks used is ®. Use of this indication is growing in the UK.

There are, of course, penalties in British law for claiming or implying registration when that is not the case or if the registered mark used is not applicable to the particular goods or circumstances.

WORDS AND PHRASES IMPORTANT TO THE SUBJECT

ASSOCIATED TRADE MARKS

It not infrequently happens that firms register variants of a trade mark. Such marks would not be separately registrable by separate owners. They are registered as 'associated marks' and as such may not be transferred at any time to separate owners. Continued use of one mark will be a defence against any suggestion of non-use of the associated marks.

DEFENSIVE TRADE MARKS

There is provision for 'the proprietors of very well-known invented-word trade marks who desire to obtain additional registrations of those marks in respect of goods for which they do not use or propose to use them'. It will be noted that this provision is very limited – 'very well known' and 'invented words'. The purpose is, of course, to provide precautionary defence for an existing trade mark. To obtain such protection it is necessary to show that, if the same or a similar mark was to be used for the additional goods specified, the public would expect manufacture of or trading in the goods to be in the hands of the original proprietor.

CERTIFICATION TRADE MARKS

'A Certification Trade Mark denotes independent certification by its owner that the goods to which it is applied possess certain defined characteristics. Registration gives exclusive rights in the use of the mark to the proprietor who may authorise others to use it in accordance with the regulation relating thereto, but who may not himself carry on a trade in the goods concerned.'[14]

Certification Trade Marks are not in the ordinary sense trade marks at all. An example is the British Standards Institution's 'Kite mark' which indicates standards for products. BSI does not, of course 'carry on a trade in the goods concerned'.

Control is divided between the Registrar of Trade Marks and the Department of Prices and Consumer Protection. Approval of such marks is dependent on the benefit likely to accrue to the public and the applicant's ability to certify the goods intended to be marked and to run the scheme. Also, and very important, it is a requirement that the opportunity should be given to all those whose products merit certification to join the scheme and to use the mark (see pages 50 and 51).

CONVENTION COUNTRIES AND CONVENTION APPLICATIONS

The UK is a party to the Paris Convention for the Protection of Industrial Property. There are reciprocal rights between the Convention countries (and some other bilateral arrangements) whereby a person who has made application to register a trade mark in a Convention country has the right, within 6 months from the date of the first application in a Convention country, to claim priority of date for applications in respect of the same mark in any other Convention country. Most of the industrialised countries of the world are parties to the Convention.

CHAPTER 6
'Passing off', slander of goods and fair trading legislation

The preceding four chapters of this book summarise the law in Britain as it concerns patents, design registration, design copyright and trade marks. In three cases – patents, design registration and trade marks – the law today is based on single Acts of Parliament which, when they were passed into law, were a progression from earlier Acts. The result was a comprehensive, up-to-date, statement. Design copyright is rather different because it is based on the 1956 Copyright Act, which provides the umbrella under which limited copyright protection is provided for industrial designs by the 1968 Design Copyright Act.

As a whole, these four bodies of legislation give protection to designers and inventors and to their supporting entrepreneurs, whether they are manufacturers or traders, in respect of their creative work. The law is, of course, subject to the interpretation of the various Acts by courts of law in the light of changing circumstances, and some interpretations have not been readily predictable. Even if the decisions made by the courts turn out in the long run to have been wise, they may still have come as a surprise to the most expert lawyers at the time they were made. Some decisions of the courts have indeed seemed to constitute important changes in the law itself, at least as it was generally understood at the time. Also, due in part to Britain's entry into the European Community, new legislation is likely to be introduced, the first example being the Patents Act, 1977.

There is, however, a further possibility for defence against some aspects of plagiarism and related abuses. It rests on a broad principle, a rule of British law, that has not been consolidated into a major Act of Parliament.

In the previous chapter about trade mark law, the fundamental point was made that the public should not be misled, should not be deceived. This same principle of law applies in a more general way to the conduct of competitive business: it is seen as wrong that a trader should practise deceit in respect of the products he markets and the way in which he markets them. Often, but by no means necessarily, it is the established firm with products and/or services of proven merit that feels that its business is suffering from unfair competition of this sort. The feeling will be that, apart from actual loss of business, the firm's goodwill is being damaged.

Blanco White[15] defines goodwill as interpreted by lawyers as 'that characteristic of a business which renders it permanent, which distinguishes an established business from one newly formed'. He goes on to say that 'in order to protect business goodwill the law forbids any trader so to conduct his trade as to mislead customers into mistaking his goods for someone else's. Nor may he mislead customers into confusing his business as a whole with someone else's. It makes no difference whether it is other traders or the general public that are deceived; nor whether the deception is fraudulent or merely mistaken or accidental; nor how it is brought about. This sort of deception is known as "passing off"; anyone who suffers financial loss as a result of it is entitled to bring an action in the courts.'

The law about 'passing off' is therefore an important part of the law about misleading business practices including, for example, using a new company name in a way that is unjustifiably similar to the name of an existing company. Some aspects of such deception will quite clearly have little to do with design. Nevertheless, the law as regards 'passing off' does provide quite wide protection against plagiarism in trade marks, company symbols, packaging of products, and even the appearance of the products themselves and the way in which services are offered. It must be said, however, that 'passing off' actions can be both difficult and expensive, and their outcome will be by no means certain. This is because it is necessary to show that the public, or the trade, had either been deceived or confused or was likely to be so by the action or business practice complained of. Actual proof of such deceit will often be difficult to provide. It will be very difficult indeed, and perhaps impossible, if the trade mark, symbol, packaging, product or service that is said to have been unfairly copied or imitated is itself new. 'Passing off' is about goodwill, and the reputation that stems from goodwill, and neither can be said to exist in respect of something that has just been introduced to the market. Protection by patent, design registration, design copyright or trade mark registration applies to new inventions, designs, works or trade marks. Such protection applies equally to established products where the term of protection is still valid. It is therefore often easier to prove an infringement than to show 'passing off'.

Not surprisingly, 'passing off' actions tend to be brought where protection cannot be or has not been obtained under more specific design protection legislation. The main purpose will be to defend company goodwill, which is itself a characteristic of the established business, product or service.

Although some business relevance is an essential element in the law of 'passing off', its ramifications stretch a long way. For example, action under 'passing off' is the means whereby professional societies are able to protect their names and initials from new organisations setting up with names and initials likely to be mistaken for them. It is also the means whereby individuals can be prevented from using affixes to which they are not entitled.

SLANDER OF GOODS – TRADE LIBEL

Another aspect of the law that deals with unfair competition in business is known as slander of goods or trade libel. It relates to false and damaging statements made from an 'indirect or dishonest motive' about another firm's goods or generally about their business which result, or are likely to result, in financial loss.

It is difficult to see any relevance in this law to protection against plagiarism in design. It is conceivable, however, that action could be taken as slander of goods if a trader were to make unwarranted criticisms in public of the design of a competitor's products with possible adverse effects on the competitor's business.

Despite the various provisions of the law which have been described, cases do remain where designers and manufacturers feel that they have suffered injustice as a result of unfair treatment of their designs or by unfair competition related to them. In some instances it may be that other considerations quite properly overrule the designer's or the manufacturer's point of view. Lawyers with experience of design matters have, however, shown much ingenuity in seeking to relate general principles of law to problems of design plagiarism. The suggestion has been made, for example, that the law concerning defamation of character might be applied to

Passing off, The Design Centre and the Design Centre Label

The name of The Design Centre is itself in no way appropriate for protection under trade mark law. As with business names generally, however, distinctiveness and goodwill have been built up to a considerable extent with the passage of years. By relying on the law concerning 'passing off' it has been possible to 'dissuade' businesses and other organisations in the UK from using the name in a way that might mislead the public and damage the success of The Design Centre.

For many years manufacturers have been able to buy or obtain a licence to use the Design Centre Label on products included in the Design Council's Design Index. Although the label is a distinctive and well established mark, it is not eligible for registration as a Part A or a Part B trade mark. This is because the goods that carry the mark are not controlled by the Design Council in the sense of being manufactured or marketed by it. The Design Centre Label is not registered as a certification trade mark either, in spite of the fact that there is a well publicised selection process. The basis for the inclusion of products in Design Index is that they should be well designed, and some of the criteria for 'good design' are not as tangibly definable as is required under the Trade Marks Act. 'Passing off' law has been quite sufficient, however, to give protection and to deter manufacturers from using the Design Centre Label when they are not entitled to do so, or from using similar marks, even if the similarity is inadvertent.

cases where a well-known product design, no longer protected by registration or copyright, has been reproduced in such an inferior way as to bring possible discredit on the name of the original designer. A graphic designer may similarly feel that inferior work, which derives from his ideas but which cannot be said to infringe his copyright, may still be damaging to his reputation. To rub salt into the wound, the new author will be entitled to copyright on the work thought to be derivative and inferior (see also pages 82 and 109).

Weights and Measures Act 1963
Food and Drugs Act 1955
Trade Descriptions Act 1968
Fair Trading Act 1973

All the legislation referred to earlier in this book has been a matter of civil law. The Acts listed above fall into the field of criminal law. The practices they were introduced to regulate or prevent were seen as being so strongly against the public interest as to be criminal and to necessitate strong countermeasures and the setting up of enforcement authorities.

These Acts all have some design relevance, but their general purpose is the regulation of trade and the protection of the consumer. None of the Acts is directly concerned with design protection. Their relevance to designers arises in the main from their requirements regarding packaging and publicity material. The principle is clear enough – that the consumer should be protected against fraudulent or unfair trading practices and misleading packaging or advertising. Detailed regulations under the Acts are made to ensure these desirable results and they need careful study.

The enforcing authorities are: Local Authority Weights and Measures Inspectors (with some responsibility to the Department of Trade); and the Office of Fair Trading, which is ministerially responsible to the Secretary of State for Prices and Consumer Protection.

CHAPTER 7
Especially for manufacturers

The first piece of advice in this chapter may seem surprising in view of the title of the book. It is that manufacturers should never allow themselves to become so obsessed by the need for design protection as to neglect design development. The prospect of protection by law for existing designs should not tempt producers into a policy of resting on hard-won design laurels. If that is done it is quite certain that trading decline will set in sooner or later. Indeed in some industries it may be that the best policy, when successful designs are being copied, is to accept the fact and to move on to new products. Once design leadership has been achieved it can never be maintained by defensive measures alone. Leadership in design, as in everything else, means keeping one jump ahead of all the others.

But this admirable philosophy cannot possibly be applied in a general way across the whole of modern industry. In many industries, even if an endless succession of good new designs were possible, the result of constant change would inevitably be that none of the designs could be fully exploited for quantity production. Furthermore, customers would become thoroughly dissatisfied as a result of the impossibility of getting replacement parts or repeat quantities. And again, some patents and trade marks – and even some designs – are so very important as to make it plain foolishness for their proprietors not to defend them to the uttermost, with a view to extracting the maximum return from their ownership rights.

WAYS OF COMBATING PLAGIARISM
WITHOUT GOING TO LAW

Before going on to discuss the action manufacturers should take in respect of design protection by law, there are some non-legal possibilities that should be considered. Earlier in this book the arguments were set down in favour of protection by law for the designer and the innovator against the plagiarist. The strongest argument was seen as being the likelihood that the country's industry and trade would be damaged if innovators were allowed to become discouraged. And discouraged they certainly would become if the results of their creative work and risk taking were exploited by others who had themselves contributed nothing.

This argument is valid for industry in general, but its implications are even more telling when applied to individual firms and particular industries. The problem is not new; referring to the revolution in manufacturing methods during the nineteenth century – the change to 'wholesale reproduction on an industrial scale' – A. D. Russell-Clarke[17] said that copying on the scale that then became possible 'could cut severely into the business of the designer (or manufacturer). It might also do him additional injury if, as often occurred, the copies were offered for sale at a lower price. A still further injury might be inflicted if the copies were inferior in quality since this inferiority might well in error be attributed by the public to the originator of the design, and thereby affect the reputation of his own goods and damage it.'

It may be that cause and effect sometimes interchange, but it is certainly a fact that the industries that are plagued by design copying are almost invariably the ones that are also plagued by price and quality cutting. Although the copyist avoids the cost of product design and development, this is rarely sufficient in itself to give him a price advantage that will enable him to secure significant business. Trade loyalty is one reason for this, but another will amost certainly be that in the process of design development, the originating company will have acquired important production know-how which their competitors will lack. The usual outcome is that the copyist will reduce quality, either of the materials used or in the weight, dimensions, colour or finish of the product. There will almost certainly also be a cut in the quality of the design itself. The imitator can be expected to show a lack of sophisticated understanding of a design in the development of which he played no part.

If such a state of affairs becomes general in an industry, the resulting loss of quality standards and design initiative will lead inevitably to a loss of reputation in overseas markets. A decline in exports will result and this will in turn be followed by growing import penetration of the home market. The

64

answer is appropriate action in good time by the relevant trade association.

A main purpose of trade associations is clearly to ensure lively, progressive, prosperous business for member firms. This can hardly result if, in industries where design is important, member firms engage in practices that nullify design initiative and lead to quality and price cutting. The action needed on the part of trade associations may simply consist of the organisation of periodic design events aimed at raising the general standard of design thinking in the industry – resulting in turn in the development among member firms of what can only be described as a reasonable standard of design morality. It may be that a panel can also be set up to advise, or even to arbitrate, on alleged instances of copying – 'getting too close' – between members.

It is obvious that there must be a limit. There must be no question of restriction of competition between members – rather the reverse. Competition at the level of encouraging design initiative will be stimulated and is greatly preferable to competition based on copying the successes of the more enterprising firms. Even so, a respectful eye should be kept on the provisions of restrictive practices legislation.

In Britain, trade associations have taken this sort of action in a number of areas, including the furniture and the carpet industries. In both cases the results have been beneficial. As an example, the British Carpet Manufacturers' Association has a Design Committee responsible to the Association Council. The Design Committee organises annual seminars for the industry's staff designers. Periodically there are tours abroad specially organised with designers' interests in mind. The committee maintains contact with art and design colleges. Problems arising from similarities between members' designs are usually settled by direct contact, but the Association has a Plagiarism Committee which serves as a forum for the consideration of complaints if necessary. The committee also takes action if member companies' designs are copied abroad. The effect of this continuing trade association initiative in the carpet industry also seems to reach out to non-member firms as well as to members.

The great majority of the designs produced by British carpet manufacturers are the work of the industry's staff designers. In the manufacture of wallcoverings it is different: a considerable proportion of the designs used are bought by manufacturers from freelance designers. The Wallcovering

Overlapping protection

As an example of the care properly taken to protect an industrial property, the Hotpoint 'Liberator De Luxe' washing-machine is covered by patents, by design registration, and by registration of relevant trade marks.

Four British patent numbers (1350911, 1414294, 1414295 and 1426076) relate to mechanical features.

Six British patent numbers (1266691, 1347675, 1353906, 1381374, 1450679 and 1450680) relate to or are associated with the clothes drum speed or acceleration control system.

One (1055587) relates to an optional feature – a connector for use with the water feed hoses.

There are two other patent applications pending.

The registered design number (960985) protects the overall appearance of the design.

The company name Hotpoint is registered as a trade mark, both in block capitals and in script form. The names 'Liberator' and 'Reversomatic' which apply to this particular machine are also registered as trade marks.

Manufacturers Association of Great Britain has accordingly taken a different and an interesting initiative. The Association, after discussions with the Society of Industrial Artists and Designers, produced a form of assignment of design copyright[18] from designers which can be used 'when commissioning a design or buying copyright in an existing design', and the wording of which may 'serve to remove occasions of difficulty or misunderstanding in the future'. The assignment is for the copyright in the design for use on wallcoverings 'throughout the world for the remainder of the term of copyright subsisting therein'. Subject to this the copyright remains with the designer. There are clauses to the effect that the designer has not sold, and will not sell in the future, the same or similar designs to other manufacturers for use on wallcoverings, and also that the designer will co-operate with the manufacturer, if requested to do so, in obtaining design registration for the design or in such measures as may be necessary to validate the copyright. The subject of such licences and assignments will be referred to again later in this and the succeeding chapter (pages 74 and 81).

An effective design committee in a trade association may also provide a partial solution to the difficult problem of design plagiarism from abroad. Action to prevent such copying will often be beyond the resources of a single company to tackle. It is at least less difficult when the industry speaks or acts together. A trade association usually has good contact with government and it can expect to be listened to. It may also approach the equivalent trade association in the other country with some hope of getting effective action.

DECISIONS ABOUT PATENTS AND REGISTRATIONS

It is very important that the law concerning patents, design registration, design copyright, trade marks, 'passing off' and so on should be seen as a whole. The first decision to make when formal design protection for a product or a design seems to be necessary is what sort of protection is relevant. It may be that there should be overlapping protection – one aspect of a product protected by patent, another by design registration, with reliance also placed on design copyright. The law is undoubtedly complex and the proper patenting of

67

an invention or the registration of a trade mark or design may be of crucial commercial and financial importance.

Specially complex circumstances may arise if an invention or a design is being licensed from abroad, or alternatively when licenses are being arranged for manufacture by other organisations, either in the UK or elsewhere.

For all these reasons it is necessary for a manufacturer to have the best possible advice. In large companies special knowledge, experience and organisation will normally have been built up. There may be a special department with a senior executive in charge; in small and medium-sized companies this is clearly not practicable. It is nevertheless advisable to have the advice of a good lawyer and contact with a patent or trade mark agent as appropriate.

ACTION IN THE EVENT OF DESIGNS BEING COPIED

In industries where the trade association affords some system of protection against plagiarism, the first action will be to contact the trade association Director or Secretary. As has already been indicated, if the facts make a good case, there may be a quick and satisfactory result.

Where it is necessary to go to law, most lawyers will say that prompt action is to be strongly recommended. If a trade mark is infringed, for example, the offender will usually have infringed out of straight ignorance and a determined protest will do the trick. If the protest proves unavailing and a good prima facie case can be urgently presented, it may be possible to obtain an injunction requiring withdrawal of the offending mark pending trial of the full action. In most cases the defending firm will then see the strength of the complainant's case, realise that they are up against a determined opponent and decide to settle.

In the case of copying involving patents and product design it may also be that an offender will plead ignorance, and a formal complaint with a show of determination will be sufficient to ensure withdrawal. A reputation for determined action against copyists can help very considerably! Court proceedings may, however, be necessary and advice may indicate the likelihood of a long and expensive fight. At this stage the decision whether or not to proceed must be essentially a commercial one. If the design that is said to have been copied is selling well, with the prospect of good future sales, it may be that the fact (and the costs) of a legal battle will be entirely acceptable. Even if the action is successful, however, it is unlikely that the costs will be wholly recoverable from the other side.

From the defendant's standpoint the merits of the case will, of course, look different. If the alleged copying cannot be disputed and if there is no doubt about the infringement – in short, if there is no defence – there can scarcely be any action. Not infrequently, however, the defendant will feel that he has a good case and then, for the defendant as for the plaintiff, basic commercial considerations will usually be dominant. Is the design complained of really succeeding? Is there potential for growth or is the competitor's product likely to keep the bulk of a limited market? If the answers to such questions are discouraging and the merits of the case seem to be nicely balanced, it may be that the battle will scarcely seem worth fighting and that a settlement should therefore be made.

THREATS

Where there appears to be infringement of patents or registered designs, their owners may feel that they should make threats of legal proceedings. They may be tempted to threaten such action, not only against the firm they see as an infringer, but also against users or stockists of the offending products.

All may be well *if* the patent or the registered design is held to be valid, and *if* the supposed offender is really infringing. But the 'ifs' are very important: the validity of the patent or the registered design may be successfully challenged, and the product complained of may be held not to be an infringement even if the validity of the protection is upheld.

The 1977 Patents Act says that 'a mere notification of the existence of a patent does not constitute a threat of proceedings within the meaning of this Section' (Section 70 of the Act).

Threats that are 'groundless', however, may themselves be the subject of legal proceedings against the person who makes them. Threats should certainly not be made, nor anything that can be construed as a threat, without careful consideration and good legal advice.

There is a different situation as regards design copyright.

The report of the Whitford Committee[2] says that 'there should be statutory prohibition in respect of unjustified threats of proceedings for infringement of copyright over the whole field of copyright, but not in respect of threats made to the primary infringer' – for example, the actual manufacturer of the offending product.

DESIGN AND DEVELOPMENT RECORDS

The passing into law of the 1968 Design Copyright Act greatly increased the importance of keeping design and development records. Whatever the nature of the design work – whether it is for three-dimensional products, pattern design for carpets, dress materials or wallcoverings, or perhaps design for business literature – in all cases drawings or models should be carefully dated, signed and kept, together with any records as to how the designs originated. Rough first sketches, notes, suggestions as to improvements, minutes of meetings – all should be kept. It has been made clear earlier in this book that design copyright turns on the act of copying, and evidence as to when and how a particular design was developed may turn out to be of much consequence. To a manufacturer whose design is copied, actual evidence of the originality of his own designers' work will be of obvious importance in any action he may bring. If the action is based on design copyright, it will be necessary to show that the product is based on drawings or a 'work of artistic craftsmanship' of acceptable date. Even if the product is protected by patent or design registration, the validity of the protection may still be challenged and evidence of the background history of the invention or design may still be necessary.

If the complaint is the other way round, and the manufacturer has to face an accusation of copying, it will still be important, if he has not copied, for him to be able to demonstrate how it came about that his designers arrived at a similar design by coincidence.

STAFF CONTRACTS AND LETTERS OF ENGAGEMENT

When staff are being engaged to be employed on research, development and design, it is important that their conditions of engagement should state their position in the event of the taking out of patents or the registration of designs, and also in respect of design copyright. Legal advice should be sought on the form of words to be used. Patent and design rights are normally vested in the employer, but the name of the individual inventor is often linked on patent specifications. This does not usually entitle the named member of staff to any monetary benefit – it would need a special agreement for him actually to share in the patent rights.

The 1977 Patents Act, however, made an important change in the law. There is provision in it for an employee to make application to the Comptroller of the Patent Office or to the court if he 'has made an invention belonging to the employer for which a patent has been granted' and if the patent is '(having regard among other things to the size and nature of the employer's undertaking) of outstanding benefit to the employer'. If the facts justify it and 'it is just that the employee should be awarded compensation to be paid by the employer, the court or the Comptroller may award him such compensation'.[7]

The bias of the law is in favour of an employee if he makes an invention that is outside the scope of his normal work. Also, the employer's rights only relate to work done during the actual period of the inventor's or the designer's employment. Before the 1977 Patents Act became effective the terms of a service agreement would generally be valid if the agreement varied the normal rules of law. The new provisions about compensation for employees' inventions apply despite such service agreements. In any case, it was not, nor is it now, permissible to enforce a service agreement that is so onerous as to prevent an inventor or designer who has left his employment from getting suitable work subsequently.

Design work in respect of corporate identity for companies or other organisations – company symbols, trade marks, trade literature – is obviously very different from inventions or product development. The application for registration of a trade mark may only be by or on behalf of the proprietor of the mark. Design copyright or other protective rights in respect of all such matters relating to a company's trading identity can be expected to become the property of the company or organisation. Nevertheless it is advisable to cover the ownership of such rights in the case of staff engaged to do graphic design work of this nature.

Although not strictly of great relevance to design

protection, an important point to cover in the engagement of staff designers is their right or otherwise to undertake additional work in a freelance capacity. If agreed, such work should not normally be allowed to involve any conflict of interest with the business of the principal employer. There is a possibility, however, that the designer's value to his main employer will be increased by reason of the greater experience and reputation he will gain by undertaking outside work.

CONTRACTS WITH CONSULTANTS

Everything said already about the necessity for a clear understanding, in written form and with a legal basis, with staff designers, applies with equal or greater force to the alternative or supplementary employment of consultant designers. There are many ways in which a consultant designer may be employed: he may be retained in a more or less permanent role, perhaps with additional payment dependent on actual work done; or he may be employed to undertake one specific task and in this case the date for delivery of the work may be particularly important. There are sometimes commission or royalty arrangements, and almost certainly payment for work done on an hourly or daily basis will allow for various grades of work at different levels of skill.

Consultant designers often work for clients for many years with full satisfaction all round; in other cases disagreements and dissatisfactions soon arise. Without doubt, in a high proportion of cases where there is an unhappy outcome, failure results from there having been no clear business understanding at the beginning.

Rights and procedures regarding design protection for work carried out should be part of such agreements. The design copyright, if intended to be vested in the employer, should be transferred from the designer to the firm along with all relevant signed and dated drawings at an appropriate time, which itself should be agreed and stated. The transfer of artwork and the payment for it do not automatically effect transfer of the copyright. The position regarding patents, design registrations or work on trade marks, symbols and other graphic design work should be similarly covered in the consultancy agreement or by exchange of letters.

photograph David Carter Associates

Design in the public sector

In accordance with their policy to facilitate open tendering, but also in order to achieve direct control over design development, the Post Office commissioned a design for a compact telephone from DCA Design Ltd, Warwick. The aim was to provide a telephone for wall mounting or table use without using separate housings. The bell and its circuitry are omitted from the base set so the telephone is smaller and lighter than usual. The user can lift the set while speaking and move about if necessary.

Two British patent numbers (1303688 and 1307870) relate to the wall mounting assembly and the terminal respectively.

There are five registered design numbers: 958481 applies to the telephone casing with dial, switch hook and base; 950242 applies to the casing alone; 947889 applies to the handset; 947891 applies to the casing of the wall mounting assembly (with patent 1303688); and 947886 applies to the casing, with base, for a separate bell set (when number 947891 is not used).

The name 'Sylphone' has been registered as a trade mark, but not used as yet.

There is a special case with freelance, as distinct from consultant, designers. In the pattern industries – particularly printed textiles and wallcoverings, but also with other design specialisations such as greeting cards and similar products in the giftware field – it is accepted practice for designers to show manufacturers portfolios of their work from which designs will be chosen. This system is by no means always satisfactory from the designer's standpoint, but manufacturers have also sometimes had grounds for complaint when inexperienced designers have been guilty of selling different, but recognisably similar, designs to manufacturers who are in competition. This was one of the reasons why the Wallcovering Manufacturers Association drew up the form of contract for the purchase of designs from freelance designers referred to earlier in this chapter (see page 65).

Another point of importance with the work of two-dimensional designers, and particularly with illustrators, is whether the design or drawing has been bought outright or whether all that has been covered is the licence to reproduce it in one or more limited contexts, the drawing itself to be returned. This should be made clear in the purchase agreement.

SECRECY UNDERTAKINGS

It is not unusual for inventors to ask manufacturers who have indicated an interest in their invention to sign a secrecy undertaking before showing them drawings, models etc. There is a further reference to this subject, which may also concern designers, in the next chapter (page 82).

DESIGNS FOR PRODUCTS FOR OPEN TENDER

It is often necessary for a new design to be developed for production subject to competitive tender. This applies particularly in the public service. Even if a manufacturer could be found who would be willing, free of charge, to allot his designers and prototype making facilities to the design work and the sample production, the situation would still be unsatisfactory. Much the best solution is for the purchasing authority to arrange a design development contract and to award it to the most appropriate designer or manufacturer.

Any patents, design registrations or design copyright that result will become the property of the purchasing authority according to the procedures laid down in the design and development contract. The specification for manufacture of the product in bulk will, of course, be issued to all those entitled to receive it and contracts can then be awarded on the basis of the best tenders received.

CHAPTER 8
Especially for designers

All the points made in the previous chapter addressed to manufacturers have relevance for designers – sometimes, of course, with the implications reversed. It may perhaps be less necessary to stress to designers the dangers of developing an unduly protective mentality about design. To most designers the main interest of the job lies in the challenge of meeting changing requirements with new design solutions. There is the constant need to move on in their own design thinking. It is still necessary, nevertheless, as with manufacturers, for them to hold a proper balance between the need to develop new designs and the commonsense requirement to take whatever steps are needed to gain the maximum commercial value from established design successes.

WAYS OF COMBATING PLAGIARISM
WITHOUT GOING TO LAW

It has been shown that manufacturers may do a great deal to limit the adverse effects of plagiarism on business through their trade associations. Designers have a parallel opportunity through membership of their professional body, the Society of Industrial Artists and Designers. Since its inception in the 1930s the SIAD has campaigned consistently against design copying. In the Society's Code of Professional Conduct,[19] under the heading 'The designer's responsibility to his fellow practitioners' is the clause 'The Society regards copying or plagiarism with intent as wholly unprofessional.' It is a condition of membership that members should abide by the code, and members failing to do so may in the last resort be expelled from the Society. The SIAD is willing to nominate expert witnesses in legal actions concerning plagiarism, and contact is maintained with other design organisations in most of the industrial countries of the world. The SIAD is a founder member of ICSID (the International Council of Societies of Industrial Design) and of ICOGRADA (the International Council of Graphic

Design Associations). It is the British member of IFI (the International Federation of Interior Designers). Instances of design copying from abroad can often be tackled through these channels.

Equally effective in the long run is the work done to raise standards of design in Britain by the Design Council, the Design and Industries Association, the Royal Society of Arts and the SIAD. If manufacturers can be helped to produce products that are better designed; if the distributive trades can be persuaded to stock and to sell well designed goods; and if the general public can be brought to demand such goods, then designers will have more scope for original work. Design copying will be less frequent and there will be less need to fall back on legal protection.

THE DESIGNER AND DESIGN PROTECTION BY LAW

As the ideal solution envisaged in the last paragraph is obviously still far from being realised, it will be seen that design protection by law is as important to the designer as it is to the entrepreneur. And if circumstances arise in which the interests of the manufacturer and the designer do not coincide, then they should both seek good legal advice.

The interests of the staff designer in any decisions about applying for patents, design or trade mark registrations, or in procedures relating to design copyright will usually be the same as those of the company for which he works. His rights will normally be vested in his employer, although his name may be linked in patents. The position of the consultant designer will depend on the terms of his consultancy agreement or exchange of letters. Whether the designer is a consultant, a freelance designer, or a member of staff of the manufacturing company, he can expect to be a key figure in any legal action, contemplated or taken, in defence of designs for which he was responsible. As the specialist on the subject his advice as to whether the design complained of should indeed be thought of as a copy will probably be the first to be sought. To most designers and manufacturers the subject of design plagiarism is a highly emotional one. The law does not go in for emotion very much so it may be useful to be objective and to bring together the points made in earlier chapters about what constitutes the act of copying.

THE ACT OF COPYING

In addition to the other differences between patent law and the law concerning design protection there also seems to be a psychological divide. It is an historical fact that many well-known inventors gained very little from the important patents they held. The profits often came later, when technical developments or market changes made mass production possible. Even so, attempts to design around a patent are usually seen as being legitimate enough (but to be opposed, of course, by the patentee where possible). Certainly when the period of protection on a patent expires, there is no stigma attaching to other manufacturers who then seek to exploit the invention – as they are fully entitled to do. Most of the emotion seems to be reserved for design copying.

If a design has been registered and the registration is still valid, there is something immediate and tangible with which to confront an infringer. The validity of the registration may, however, be challenged and the issue will then turn, as it will with design copyright, on the similarity of the two designs. But copyright is about copying, and if design copyright is to be effective there are some basic requirements: the design that is alleged to have been copied should itself be based on drawings or a 'work of artistic craftsmanship'; it should be an original work and not another copy; and sufficient skill and labour should have gone into its production to constitute it as an 'artistic work'. Manufacturers and designers may have good cause to feel that their designs have been copied, but if these basic requirements cannot be shown to have been met there is little hope of legal redress. As an example, a successful design may perhaps be based on new drawings, but be simple in style with clear antecedents in the particular industry. In such a case a similar design produced by another company will be difficult to attack, but it may help if the copyist gives the game away by slavishly incorporating character-giving elements or by using exact dimensions and construction details in a way that will stretch the credulity of anyone asked to believe that it is all coincidental.

A major question frequently to be considered will be whether what seems like copying is indeed that, or whether the alleged offender has simply been influenced in a legitimate way in producing a somewhat similar design. This is the ever-recurring problem of what is a 'fair follower' and what is not. The best guide is to consider whether the second design contributes something materially new despite being linked with the basic idea of the first. There is reference to a recent relevant court case on page 86.

It has already been said that for successful patents the end of the protection period is generally accepted as being the fair opportunity for others to exploit the invention if they think it profitable so to do. Manufacturers with a successful industrial design do not always take the same view, despite the fact that the normal run for a popular design in many industries is shorter than the life of a worthwhile invention. Some designs do have a much longer life than the 15 years protection provided by design registration or by design copyright, and the manufacturers of such designs often feel very wronged if their designs are then copied by other firms. The only remedy, if it is appropriate, is by an action for 'passing off'.

DESIGN AND DEVELOPMENT RECORDS

In the preceding chapter the importance was stressed of keeping full records to show the origin and the development of new designs. In practice, the keeping of such records will usually be the responsibility of the company's design director, design manager or, perhaps more simply, the company's designer. It is one part of the job of design management and regrettably it often tends to be taken rather lightly. It will be said that everyone appreciates the importance of keeping full design records, but the records themselves, on inspection, often seem to be haphazard and incomplete. The excuse will be given that it is only by hindsight that the really successful designs can be known, and that to record all the design histories of the company as they develop would be an impossible task. Nevertheless, systematic records should be kept. They should be fully documented, properly dated and signed – and of course well maintained.

STAFF CONTRACTS AND
LETTERS OF ENGAGEMENT

The explanations given under this heading in the previous chapter (page 70) are at least as relevant to the designer as they are to the manufacturer. (The change in the law in the

1977 Patents Act is particularly important.) When being interviewed for staff posts, designers should seek clarification of their position in respect of patents, design registrations and copyright and their eligibility or otherwise to undertake freelance, non-competitive work.

Confirmation in writing should be requested before the job is accepted.

CONSULTANT AND FREELANCE DESIGNER CONTRACTS

It is obviously equally important for consultant designers to have a clear understanding with their client firms before work is undertaken. Design protection procedures apart, most of the dissatisfactions of designers doing consultant or freelance work result from a failure to agree essential points when the job is first being negotiated.

Copyright in his work is of great potential value to a designer in respect of royalty negotiations. It should be clearly established whether a design is being produced or sold with the copyright to be assigned in all respects; or whether the agreement is only for reproduction of the design in a limited context. Dorothy Goslett[20] says that 'a designer should always retain the copyright of his designs at the preliminary design stage and, if the job proceeds, normally throughout the development stages too'. At the production stage for a three-dimensional product it is very unlikely that a client will accept that the designer should retain full copyright unless the circumstances are exceptional. 'But restricted copyright often applies in sections of graphic and applied design. If you are going to design a poster you would agree to convey restricted copyright to your client which would mean that he could not use it for, say an advertisement or brochure cover without negotiating further fees with you for such extended reproduction rights. A printed textile design might have restricted copyright to prevent it being used for a wallpaper without further fees for the designer.'[20]

However the copyright situation is resolved, the designer will still be interested in his design. He may feel that he should work out the colourways; he will usually expect to be consulted about possible modifications to meet technical or marketing requirements; he will certainly be expected to co-operate with his client in any way deemed necessary to

81

protect his designs. These points should not be taken for granted. They should be discussed and if possible they should be covered in the initial agreement. Failing that they should be dealt with in a subsequent exchange of letters.

'DROIT MORAL' – the designer's moral rights

Having sold a design and assigned the copyright on it, a designer will usually feel, for the sake of his own reputation, that he should retain some rights in the way it is reproduced. 'The designer has always sought protection against plagiarism... but also against unauthorised alterations and possible mutilations of his work... English law provides three distinct forms of protection against unauthorised commercial exploitation: patents, registered designs and copyright, but remains relatively unconcerned with what is recognised in other jurisdictions as the "droit moral"... the right to claim authorship of the work, sometimes called the right of paternity, and the right to object to any distortion or modification of the work if this prejudices the author's honour or reputation, sometimes called the right of integrity. The only similar provision in English law is section 43 of the Copyright Act 1956 which makes the false attribution of authorship actionable. As can be seen from its history English industrial property law has concerned itself almost wholly with the protection of economic interests.'[21]

The designer's contract with his client is, therefore, all the more important.

SECRECY UNDERTAKINGS

As mentioned earlier (page 74) inventors sometimes ask manufacturers to sign a secrecy undertaking before they show them the drawings, models etc relating to their invention with a view to its manufacture. Such undertakings require confidentiality on the part of the firm, and its employees, in all matters concerning the invention should the firm decide not to proceed. A period of time may be given for proper consideration together with a first option for manufacture.

The same procedure may very well be applicable to designers when their design has been developed independently and they are seeking a manufacturer who will undertake commercial production.

One advantage is that the wording of the undertaking can cover the idea for the product which could certainly not be protected by design registration or design copyright. Secrecy undertakings need careful legal drafting.

TAXATION

There are special rules regarding patents and Income Tax. The explanatory booklet issued by the Board of Inland Revenue[22] explains that 'expenditure and receipts in respect of patents may be either of an income or a capital nature'. Royalties or other sums paid by the user of a patent for restricted rights, and where there is no element in the arrangement that can be regarded as purchase of the property of the patent, are treated as income. Certain reliefs may be claimed.

Other payments, including payments for outright acquisition or exclusive use (perhaps within a defined area) for the unexpired life of the patent or for a period of years, are generally treated as capital. Such payments may qualify for Income Tax allowances for the payer and are taxed as income of the recipient. Capital sums received in this way may be treated as income spread over a six year period.

There are no special rules for treatment of income from registered designs and designs protected by copyright. If receipts arise in the course of carrying on a trade or profession, they will be included in the profits assessable under Case I or Case II of Schedule D. Otherwise the receipts will be assessable under Case VI of Schedule D.

Where copyright is assigned on an artistic work and the author was engaged on it for more than a year he may, for income tax purposes, spread the payments he receives over two years (or three if the time spent on the work exceeds two years). The spread for tax purposes will be by dating back – one half (or one third) in each of two (or three) years. The arrangement also applies when an artist 'was engaged for a period of more than 12 months in making a number of works of art for an exhibition and the work (sold or commissioned) is one of them'.[23]

PARTICULAR CASES

ARTISTIC WORKS
Before considering categories of design it will be useful to clarify the position as regards works of art. The Copyright

Act 1956 makes the proviso that such works shall be 'original' and defines 'artistic work' as being '(a) . . . irrespective of artistic quality . . . paintings, sculptures, drawings, engravings and photographs; (b) works of architecture, being either buildings or models of buildings; (c) works of artistic craftsmanship, not falling within either of the preceding paragraphs.' Works in these three sectors have copyright protection for 50 years from the end of the year in which the author dies (this provision is varied in respect of engravings and photographs). There are definitions of the individual words – 'sculptures', 'drawings', 'photographs', 'works of architecture' etc – either as they are included in the Copyright Act or as they have arisen from court rulings, and these are to be found in Russell-Clarke.[9]

It should be noted that works of architecture and works of artistic craftsmanship are *not* protected 'irrespective of artistic quality'.

Commissioning complicates the ownership of copyright in most of these areas of 'artistic work', but there is a special point about architecture which should be mentioned. An architect not in full-time staff employment normally retains the copyright in the plans drawn for his clients despite having been paid for them. He also has copyright in the buildings built from them unless something special has been arranged.

This has two basic results: the architect can make further use of his work, if it is appropriate, when making plans for other buildings; and the owner of the building cannot erect duplicates of his building without the consent of the owner of the copyright – the architect. The consent may, of course, be linked with a fee and a further commission to do the work necessary in modifying the plans for the other building or buildings required.

Two Court of Appeal cases,[24][25] however, seem to establish the principle that if an architect has been paid the normal fee up to a recognised stage in the design process, according to the RIBA scale, there is an implied licence to proceed. The owner of the projected building (or, for that matter, the architect) may terminate the engagement on payment of the appropriate fees and on the expiry of reasonable notice. The client may employ a builder (or another architect) to use the plans 'for that very building on that site, but for no other purpose'.[24]

The current RIBA Conditions of Engagement[26] were not

in force for the cases quoted. Today's conditions make a distinction between Stage C (Outline Proposals) and Stage D (Scheme Design). From Stage D onwards 'the client, unless otherwise agreed shall, on payment or tender of any fees due to the architect, be entitled to reproduce the design . . . but only on the site to which the design relates'. Up to and including the earlier Stage C, 'the client may not reproduce the design by proceeding to execute the project without the consent of the architect and payment of any additional fee that may be agreed in exchange for the architect's consent'.[26] There is provision that the architect 'shall not unreasonably withhold his consent', arbitration is seen as possible and, generally, so are special agreements.

CATEGORIES OF DESIGN

For reference purposes the classification is that developed by the SIAD.[27] Repetition of the general principles explained in the earlier chapters of this book is avoided as much as possible. There is a varying amount of detail from category to category because there have not been significant court cases in all areas.

A–   *Product Design*
A1   *Engineering Products*
A2   *Industrialised Building Systems*

Engineering products, whether capital goods equipment or domestic products, are clearly a prime area for overlapping design protection: patents for the mechanisms and the electrical or electronic systems etc by which they operate; design registration for aspects of the product design that are registrable; design copyright for non-registrable, but still original, elements of their design. Products may be further protected by registration of the trade names and trade marks under which they are sold (see pages 42 and 43). When there is a long development stage for a product, registration is desirable for the interim design used for showing to potential suppliers of component parts and on marketing trials. If the designer is a member of the manufacturer's staff, the copyright in his drawings will normally be vested in his employer. If he is a consultant, copyright will usually be retained during the development stages and assigned when the completion fees are paid.

There are areas of product design that overlap with

architecture. In its submission of evidence to the Whitford Committee,[2] the SIAD argued that copyright protection should be made more consistent as between the two areas. The Society instanced domestic greenhouses as a category in which it claimed there had in recent years been new designs showing a 'significant creative contribution'. It said: 'Clearly these are buildings, if small ones. They are also industrial products and while it is possible that they have been designed by architects it is more likely that they are the work of an industrial designer.' It was explained that 'protection could be sought under provisions relating to works of architecture' or, by following precedents in recent cases, 'on the protection afforded to designs embodied in drawings'.[28]

A3 Furniture
A4 Ceramics
A5 Glass
In all three areas there is full artistic copyright protection for the designer/craftsman producing 'works of artistic craftsmanship' as unique pieces or in small numbers. However, as has been noted previously, the words 'irrespective of artistic quality', which specifically apply to paintings, sculptures, drawings etc, do not apply to 'works of artistic craftsmanship'. The law in this area is unclear and it cannot be assumed, for example, that copyright could be claimed on pieces of craft pottery showing no original thought. Also, although the '50 rule' applies, it cannot be assumed that the designer/craftsman in furniture could claim artistic copyright protection if he were to delegate the making of 49 of the 50 pieces to assistants. He would have much better claim to design copyright protection for 15 years under the 1968 Act based on drawings or on his own original 'work of artistic craftsmanship'.

For the industrial manufacturer of furniture, ceramics or glass, design protection is possible by patent, by registered design or by design copyright. In all three industries, although there may be drawings, it is likely that the design development will be heavily dependent on making prototypes. In an important case[13] it was clear that the courts insist on the meaning of the two words 'artistic' and 'craftsmanship' being fully met and united in the same person if the prototype is to provide the basis for copyright.

A more recent case[29] turned on what constitutes copying.

The case went to the Court of Appeal whose decision reversed that of the lower court.

The case concerned the design of plastics knock-down drawers for the furniture industry. The two makes of drawer were, for trade reasons, virtually identical in their dimensions. It was admitted that the second design had been produced in full knowledge of the first and as a potential replacement for it. The lower court granted 'a perpetual injunction restraining the defendant from infringing the plaintiff's copyright...'.

The Court of Appeal, in reversing the judgement, found that although the defendant had used the idea embodied in the plaintiff's design, the actual design had not been copied except in one respect, which was not seen as being sufficiently material to affect their judgement. The judgement includes the following explanatory passage: 'The similarity (of the two designs) is, in our view, a natural consequence of the defendant having adopted the concept of the plaintiff's design. This the defendant was fully entitled to do, provided that the plaintiff's design was not actually copied to any substantial extent. There was nothing reprehensible in the defendant producing something very like the plaintiff's drawer so long as the defendant did not make use of the skill and labour expended by the plaintiff in producing the designs for that drawer in which copyright is claimed by copying any substantial part of them.'[29]

A6 Jewellery
A7 Silver and Cutlery

Again there is full artistic copyright protection for the designer/craftsman, with the same qualifications as for furniture, ceramics and glass concerning the need for both artistic quality, involving original thought, and personal involvement in the craftsmanship.

Inexpensive jewellery is an industry that has been very much subject to design copying, often from abroad. The industry was one of those that pressed for a form of automatic copyright protection on the grounds that design registration was too slow, too costly, and in the case of inexpensive jewellery, often not available because the designs were too close to natural forms. (This is referred to more fully in the next section concerning toys.) The result was the 1968 Design Copyright Act.

Hallmarking is *not* a form of design protection. It has, however, some relevance to the subject. Also, hallmarks relate in certain ways to Certification Trade Marks.

The hallmark can be seen primarily as giving consumer protection and it dates from around 1300. It is a series of punched symbols denoting that the 'ware' has been tested for quality of alloy at one of the four assay offices in the UK and it is up to one of the legal 'standards'. There are four marks in the case of silver and platinum and five for gold. They are:

The Maker's or Sponsor's Mark. Usually the company or person's initials.

The Date Letter. A different letter of the alphabet is used for each year. The style of letter or background shield is changed on the completion of a cycle.

Assay Office Mark. This symbol shows which assay office – London, Birmingham, Sheffield or Edinburgh – tested the ware.

The Quality Marks. Silverware has a lion passant for sterling silver (lion rampant in Scotland) and the figure of Britannia for Britannia silver. All gold articles now have a crown and the standard is given in figures showing the number of parts of fine gold per 1000 parts of alloy. Before 1975 the standard was denoted by the 'carat' figures (22, 18, 14 or 9) and the crown was only used on 18 and 22 carat articles. The decimal equivalent (0·585 or 0·375) was used on the two lower standards.

Platinum is hallmarked by an orb as the standard mark denoting 950 parts of platinum per 1000.

Hallmarking is controlled by the Hallmarking Act 1973 and under its provisions 'British hallmarks are protected from counterfeiting or transposing and the assay offices also have the power to obliterate or cancel any mark of the character of a hallmark which an article coming into their custody or possession has and which the assay office are satisfied (a) has not been struck thereon by an assay office according to law or (b) is not a true description because the article appears to have been the subject of an improper alteration'.[30]

Other countries have different systems, but most foreign, gold, silver and platinum articles, if described as such in the course of trade or business in Britain must also be hallmarked at one of the four British assay offices or bear 'Convention' marks applied at an authorised assay office in a country which is a member of the International Hallmarking Convention.

The authorised marks are registered with the World Intellectual Property Organisation.

A8 Toys, souvenirs, travel goods and giftware

All these industries can be said to be very subject to changes in fashion leading to spurts in demand and sometimes to relatively short production runs. Protection by design copyright, being automatic and immediate, seems generally to have been advantageous.

The toy industry had a direct concern in one of the best remembered of copyright actions, which centred on 'Popeye the Sailor'.[31] The original cartoon figure appeared in an American newspaper and then in films. The author gave no authority for the character to be industrially produced as toys or brooches, but it was so produced and proved to be popular. It was eventually held that the author was entitled to artistic copyright protection since there was no intention on his part to use the design as a subject for industrial manufacture when he created it. The 'Popeye case' established the right of artists who develop characters for cartoons, comics, films and television to the full term of artistic copyright – life plus 50 years.

Before 1968 designs based on such characters, if applied industrially (under licence from the author) were eligible for design registration. Since 1968 automatic protection by design copyright is, of course, also possible, the term in both cases being 15 years.

The toy and giftware industries were strong supporters of the case for design copyright protection, which culminated in the passing into law of the 1968 Design Copyright Act. One of the reasons was that many of their designs were, and still are, representational or naturalistic in character – model cars, aircraft, toy soldiers and designs based on flowers, birds, animals and insects. Such designs could not be protected by design registration. The 1968 Act gave protection against copying by design copyright.

A9 Sport goods, boats and sailing equipment

Technical and design advances in these industries are sporadic, but very significant when they occur. Patents are sometimes appropriate, but may seem expensive relative to the sales possible; designs can be registered and design copyright can be very important. A notable court case[11] related to the design of a sailing dinghy. All parties agreed that the completed hull of the dinghy could have been registered as a design. It was not registered, however, and it was held that neither the plans nor the kit of parts from which a complete boat could be built were registrable. The designer could therefore rely on the full term of artistic copyright in respect of the plans. The defendants were held to have infringed the designer's copyright by making the parts from which a complete boat could be assembled and also by making and selling complete dinghies.

This case came before the passing into law of the 1968 Design Copyright Act. Under that Act a design for a sailing dinghy when 'applied industrially' – that is, sold as manufactured boats – has protection for 15 years. This is not felt to be very long for 'class boats', which sometimes have a much longer life. However, there may be other complications for the 'pirate' builder which are unconnected with the law. The copyright for national and international classes is often assigned as appropriate to either the Royal Yachting Association or the International Yacht Racing Union which in turn control the licensing of builders. Most Class Associations are affiliated to the RYA (which has links with the IYRU), so purchasers of boats from non-licensed builders may find it difficult to get registered sail numbers!

Some designers of sailing dinghies do not wish to assign their copyright to the RYA or the IYRU. If they retain the full copyright in their drawings when licensing their designs to builders, they should, in principle, strengthen their position in respect of royalty payments.

The sailing dinghy case referred to above has had important implications in other industries where plans and kits of parts may constitute important business.

Drawings and plans for larger boats (and ships) and for their interior design are covered by copyright in the normal way.

B–   *Fashion/Textile Design*
B16   *Dress and Fashion*
B17   *Dress accessories*
B18   *Footwear*

This is the prime area for different opinions (and fierce arguments) as to what constitutes a 'fair follower'. There are two principles: first, design protection, whether by registration or by copyright, is *not* protection for ideas, however original – the protection afforded by law is protection for designs, for specific works; and second, protection by copyright turns on the act of copying – copying the actual design, the specific work in a substantial way. (Minor amendments to the design will not free the copyist from infringement.).

Haute couture designs, being either unique or produced in very small numbers, can be expected to have artistic copyright protection – life plus 50 years – based on drawings or the 'work of artistic craftsmanship'.

There is, however, an interesting case[32] which turned on whether, and in what circumstances, a dress could be counted as a 'work of artistic craftsmanship'. The designer had done sketches which might have met today's requirements under the 1968 Act. As to the making up of the dress from the drawings, the judge found that all that the firm's 'workwomen' had done was 'to do certain acts of craftsmanship'. They had produced the dress 'by purely mechanical means'. 'They are craftswomen, but they are not artistic craftswomen; they borrowed the artistic qualities of the article from the inspiration' of the designer in her sketch. Accordingly, the made up dress was *not,* in the judge's view, 'an original work of artistic craftsmanship because the artistic element did not originate in those who made the work'.

It may be very unimportant whether an expensive dress should have copyright protection for life plus 50 years as a 'work of artistic craftsmanship' or only for 15 years based on drawings and the 1968 Design Copyright act. It is very important, however, that a dress designer should be able to show evidence of his original inspiration by having detailed, clearly understandable, dated drawings. Alternatively, if he relies on a model dress as a 'work of artistic craftsmanship' he should have had real personal involvement in its making as well as in its design.

Although the case mentioned above dates from 1936 its current importance was borne out in a more recent judgement on an application for an interlocutory injunction.[33] The injunction was granted, it being held 'that there was a serious case to be argued and that the balance of convenience lay in favour of the plaintiffs' who had alleged infringement of copyright in respect of 'three stages of their manufacturing procedure, namely design sketches, cutting patterns and prototype garments'. The recognition of copyright potential, not only in the design sketches, but also in the drawings for cutting patterns and in the prototype garments, makes this judgement an encouraging one for designers in dress and fashion.

B19   Textiles, printed
B20   Textiles, woven
B24   Textiles, knitted
B21   Rugs and carpets
B22   Wallpapers
B23   Laminates and synthetic fabrics

Since design copyright of industrially produced products is based on copyright in the original drawings, the definition of 'drawings' is very important. The definition (in the 1956 Copyright Act) is wide – 'includes any diagram, map, chart or plan' – and it is not exhaustive. In a recent case[34] it was held that a pattern made initially on point paper (graph paper in non-textile terms) is a 'drawing' within the meaning of the Act.

Craftsman handloom weavers, and designers for woven materials to be produced industrially, often design 'on the loom'. They do not always produce an initial sketch on paper and they may not have an initial point paper plan. Their claim to copyright in their work may be based on their samples being 'works of artistic craftsmanship', with the usual requirement that the full meaning of both words shall have been met. They will be well advised also to keep sketches or point paper plans.

There is a reference to freelance designers and restricted copyright for textile and wallpaper designs on page 81. The recommended form of assignment of copyright worked out between the Wallcovering Manufacturers' Asssociation of Great Britain and the SIAD is described on page 65.

C31   Exhibitions
C32   Display and display accessories
C33   Shops and shop fittings
C34   Domestic, commercial and industrial interiors
C35   Decorative building materials
C36   Television, film and theatre sets

Design copyright in all these cases will be based on copyright in the original drawings, supported in all probability by models. (Some of these categories overlap with architecture and 'models of buildings' are specifically included in the 1956 Act as 'artistic works'.) If the designer is a member of staff of the organisation or firm for which the work is being done, his rights will normally be vested in his employer.

If the exhibition, display or interior designer is freelance, it is normal for the designer to retain full copyright in his designs, the arrangement being for one use only of the exhibition, exhibition stand or interior and any related equipment that he has designed. If the exhibition is to tour, or the display to be mounted simultaneously in several shops, this should be covered in the agreement made about fees before the job is undertaken. In practice, of course, most touring exhibitions have to be redesigned in some degree to fit varied sites. The extent of the work involved in such redesigning may not be immediately appreciated by some clients.

Copyright in relation to photography will be referred to later (page 97), but the subject must also be mentioned here. Many exhibitions, displays and designs for commercial interiors make extensive and important use of photographs. In general, the copyright of a photograph is the property of the owner of the negative. He must be contacted, the proposed use explained, and a fee or caption credit may be required. Some photographers ask that they should prepare any enlargements required themselves (they may make it a condition of agreeing to the photograph being used). Sometimes, exhibition designers (with the agreement of the copyright owner) use photographs in a creative way to produce what is, in effect, a new image. A second copyright then applies.

A problem arises in relation to exhibitions where it is intended to show inventions that are new but have not yet been patented, and designs that are new but have not been registered. The inclusion of such items in an exhibition open to the trade or public constitutes 'publication' and will invalidate possible subsequent application for a patent or a design registration. To obviate this to some extent, it was possible under the 1949 Acts for application to be made to the Department of Trade (Industrial Property and Copyright Department) for a certificate which would be shown in the exhibition. The effect of the certificate was to give exhibitors six months from the date of the opening of the exhibition in which to apply for the grant of a patent or for registration of the design. The exhibition organisers would then notify the intending exhibitors of the prototype work who thus had cover (in the UK) for a limited period while they made up their minds whether to proceed with a formal application.

The 1977 Patents Act only provides for such cover in respect of patent applications if the inventions are shown at international exhibitions and certificates to that effect are obtained at the exhibition. The provision in respect of design registration still stands, but may be thought to be less important since design copyright is unaffected in such circumstances, copyright on the basic drawings being automatic and not invalidated by publication.

The terms of their contracts are very important to theatre, film and television designers working freelance and they will usually be well advised to entrust their affairs to a theatrical agent. The theatrical world is accustomed to dealing with actors through their agents, so it is not surprising that the same system should be advantageous for designers. As a result of its central role a theatrical agency may prove to be essential for finding jobs, expert in negotiating fees and alive to the importance of securing proper credits for the designer.

The theatre designer should not normally assign his work to the theatre company (his drawings may themselves be valuable). He should license his designs on a one-location, one-run basis with the integrity of his designs and proper programme credits guaranteed. He should seek the right to additional fees should the show go on tour at home or abroad, or move from one theatre to another.

With films the principles are similar, but much greater sums of money are usually involved, contracts tend to be more detailed in setting out the rights of the parties, and the scene is a much more international one.

In television a high proportion of the designers are full-time employees of their television companies (BBC or independent). The copyright of their work is, of course, vested in their employing organisations. Designers working freelance assign or license the copyright in their drawings to the company on payment of the agreed fee. Actors (and more recently directors) get a 'residual' (repeat fee) if a pro-gramme is repeated. Such fees have not yet been agreed for designers, but credits are more freely given for both staff and freelance designers than was the case at one time.

D   Graphic Design

Rule 26 para 3 in support of the Registered Designs Act 1949 specifically excluded from registration 'Printed matter primarily of a literary or artistic character, including bookjackets, calendars, certificates, coupons, dressmaking patterns, greetings cards, leaflets, maps, plans, postcards, stamps, trade advertisements, trade forms and cards, transfers and the like'.

Being excluded from design registration, this extensive but not exhaustive range of graphic design work became eligible for the full term of artistic copyright protection and this was not affected by the Design Copyright Act 1968.

D46   Typography
D47   Lettering and calligraphy

In years past, type-faces have been registrable as designs, and designs for individual letters are still registrable under the 1949 Registered Designs Act if they meet the requirement for novelty. There is a problem, however, with founts of designs: 'The individual letters may, and usually will, possess a harmony which runs through the fount and is characteristic of it, but the practice of the Patent Office since about 1939 has been to hold that this harmony does not satisfy the requirements for a set.'[2]

The 1962 Johnston Committee recommended that protection should be given by ordinary copyright law to 'every original set of lettering',[1] and proposed appropriate amendments to the Copyright Act 1956. The proposed amendments have not been made, but the report of the Whitford Committee in 1977 notes that 'The Johnston recommendations were, of course, made before the enactment of the Design Copyright Act 1968. In the United Kingdom, it is now probable that, so far as that Act is concerned, type-faces enjoy a period of 15 years protection after their first industrial manufacture. But some doubt has been expressed as to whether a set of lettering, as opposed to the individual letters, qualifies as an artistic work within the meaning of the Copyright Act 1956.'[2]

The recommendation of the Whitford Committee is that 'The Johnston Committee recommendations on the protection of type-faces should be implemented and the United Kingdom should ratify the Vienna Agreement on the Protection of Type Faces. The term of protection should be 25 years. Normal copyright rules should apply.'[2]

A further point about typography is that copyright exists in respect of books, not only in the literary sense but also for their design – their typographical and layout quality. Copyright in this second sense is the property of the publisher, it is for 25 years and it is a safeguard against reproduction by copying by whatever means.

D48   Publicity material
D49   Television and film graphics
The principle of restricted copyright has already been explained in relation to consultant and freelance designers' contracts (page 81). There is a further possibility for restricted copyright in the case of publicity material for use in newspapers and magazines. Advertisements and editorial features involving design, originally intended for use in local publications may, if successful, subsequently be used nationally or even internationally. If the designer has covered this point by assigning his copyright for a specified limited use, he should be entitled to additional fees when his work is given wider circulation.

Designers working on publicity material, ranging from books to the simplest of brochures and other advertising material, have to cope in much the same way as exhibition designers with copyright of any photographs they want to use (page 93). Copyright is normally the property of the owner of the negative and a fee may have to be paid for use of the photograph. Alternatively the owner may be pleased just to have a credit.

D50   Trade marks and symbols
D51   Packaging
It would be most unusual for full copyright not to be assigned to the firm or the organisation for whom the work has been done once the full fee has been paid.

D52   Fashion illustration
D53   General illustration
D54   Technical illustration
D55   Cartoons
In all these cases the drawings will rank as 'artistic work' with full life plus 50 years copyright protection. The question of restriction of licence will obviously be important and there are several variables – restriction relative to specific use, to re-use in another context, to possible reprints, and to

circulation. If the artist/designer assigns full copyright, he will not be entitled to the return of his original drawing.

The 'Popeye saga' referred to in respect of the toy and giftware industries has obvious relevance (page 89).

D56 Photography

Copyright on photographs has already been referred to twice (pages 93 and 96). Photographs are specifically included in the definition in the 1956 Copyright Act as being 'artistic works'. Copyright, exceptionally, (although engravings are treated in a very similar way) is for 50 years from the date of publication of the photograph. If unpublished, a photograph remains in copyright in perpetuity. Copyright is, of course, in the work – the actual photograph – and not in the subject matter of the photograph. In theory, the thousands of people who take photographs from, say, the Rialto Bridge, all have copyright in their particular 'work', but none of them have copyright on views from the Rialto Bridge.

With photographs, copyright gives protection against their reproduction, without permission, by whatever means – including someone painting a picture from the photograph. In general, copyright goes with the ownership of the negative. (The Act says that 'the author of a photograph is the owner of the material on which it was taken when it was taken'.) When photographs are commissioned there are complications and the coincidence of ownership of the negative and ownership of the copyright will be dependent on a number of variables in the commissioning arrangement.

The Whitford Committee[2] found that 'photographers today are apparently faced with the position that, in many cases, they have to work with material which is not their property, for some clients insist upon their work being done with materials supplied by their clients'. The Committee also heard evidence to the effect that the 'photographer' was not necessarily 'the person releasing the shutter, but rather the person responsible for "organising" the taking of the photograph'. Accordingly, the recommendation of the Whitford Committee was that 'the author of a photograph should be defined as the person responsible for the composition of the photograph'.[2]

CHAPTER 9
Design protection in other countries

ORGANISATION WORLDWIDE

The law in Britain concerning patents, design protection, trade marks and business practice has developed gradually over the centuries. Despite all the efforts of legislators to rationalise it and to amend it as circumstances have changed, it is still far from simple. The international position in respect of the same subjects is understandably even more difficult. Different countries have legal systems that are based on different principles; they have different attitudes to the ethics of trading; and they are at different stages of industrialisation.

The growth of world trade does, however, have a unifying influence as well as being potentially beneficial for all. For very many years, therefore, forces have been at work seeking to achieve greater co-operation between the nations as regards protection for inventions and designs. A very important aspect is the attempt to reduce the costs of taking out patents, and registering designs and trade marks, in a number of countries, by creating machinery for multinational protection based on a single application to an international authority.

WORLD INTELLECTUAL PROPERTY ORGANISATION (WIPO)

The United Nations' answer to the problem was to establish the World Intellectual Property Organisation (WIPO) as one of its special agencies in 1974. Its headquarters are in Geneva and it was actually founded in 1970 with its beginnings still earlier in the Paris Convention of 1883. Its membership of 73 states includes almost all the industrialised countries of the world (the major country missing is the People's Republic of China). In addition to inventions, industrial designs, trade marks and copyright, WIPO is also concerned with the repression of unfair competition – the repression of 'acts of competition contrary to honest practices in industrial or commercial matters'.[3] The secretariat of WIPO is known as the International Bureau and it administers the 'Unions' based on a number of international conventions.

PARIS CONVENTION FOR THE PROTECTION OF INDUSTRIAL PROPERTY, 1883

The International Union to which the convention relates has 87 member states (including the UK). The convention applies to inventions, trade marks, service marks, industrial designs, trade names, indications of origin and unfair competition. There are 'common rules' concerning laws in individual countries and 'as regards the protection of individual property, each contracting state must grant the same protection to nationals of other contracting states as it grants to its own nationals'.[3] The convention also provides for 'right of priority' in respect of patents, trade marks and industrial designs. On the basis of a first application filed in one of the member countries, an applicant may apply within a certain period for protection in any of the other member countries, such applications counting as if they had been filed on the same day as the first application. This priority advantage has, of course, no relevance under an automatic copyright system.

The Paris Convention leaves individual member countries with considerable flexibility as to legislation concerning the scope, method, duration, and nature of the industrial property protection provided. Member states may conclude separate special agreements to carry inter-member co-operation further forward.

The agreements or treaties so far concluded are:

MADRID AGREEMENT OF 1891
For the repression of false or deceptive indications of source of goods in 32 states (including the UK).

MADRID AGREEMENT OF 1891
Concerning the international registration of trade and service marks in 24 states (not including the UK).

This important agreement was last revised in 1967. Those applying for registration of their marks must have a firm base in one of the member countries and must first register their mark in that country. Firms may then apply through their national office to the International Bureau for 'international registration' – potentially, registration which will be effective, after publication by WIPO, in all 24 member countries. Each country has, however, an option to refuse registration. The advantage offered is that, after registration in the applicant's country of origin, registration is possible in a wide spread of countries based on one application, one fee, one language (French) and the same again for renewal (after 20 years).

'The UK has never adhered to the Madrid Agreement for two main reasons. One, that with registration in the applicant's home or business country as the first requirement, the system is more helpful to nationals of countries with a partial examination or deposit register than it is to the nationals of a country such as the UK where time is required for a full search and thorough examination. Second, the fee structure is such that the allocations to countries making a full search and thorough examination do not cover that work so that foreign applicants have to be subsidised by the home traders.'[16]

Possible revisions led to proposals for the Trade Mark Registration Treaty (TRT) to be referred to later (page 103).

HAGUE AGREEMENT OF 1925
Concerning the international deposit of industrial designs in 15 states (not including the UK).

The report of the Whitford Committee says that the Hague Agreement 'provides a method by which, on a single registration in Geneva, it is possible to obtain protection in a number of countries party to the treaty. In other words registration in Geneva counts as if an application has been made in each of the member countries. Each country has the right to refuse (within a given period) in accordance with the terms of its domestic law, but, in the absence of such refusal, the design is prima facie protected in each for a minimum of 10 years.'[2]

The report goes on to say that if a deposit system for the protection of designs, not involving a search for novelty were to be 'adopted in this country for some, or all, categories of designs there would appear to be a case for the United Kingdom considering joining the Hague Agreement'.[2]

NICE AGREEMENT OF 1957
Concerning the international classification of goods and services for the purposes of the registration of trade and service marks in 31 states (including the UK).

LISBON AGREEMENT OF 1958
For the protection of appelations of origin and their international registration in 15 states (not including the UK).

LOCARNO AGREEMENT OF 1968
Establishing an international classification for industrial designs in 16 states (not including the UK).

PATENT CO-OPERATION TREATY (PCT), WASHINGTON, 1970
(Including the UK.)
'The Treaty provides for the filing of an "international application" where protection is sought for an invention in several countries . . . Filing of such applications will have the same effect as if applications had been filed separately in each of the countries in which protection is desired. The international application will then be subjected to a search to discover 'prior art' and also, if specially requested by the applicant, to a preliminary examination to find out whether the invention seems to be new, non-obvious, and industrially applicable. Once the relevant reports have been established – and not before – the application will be processed separately in the various countries, each of which will then grant or refuse protection.'[3]

It is claimed that the procedure will have great advantages to the applicant because it will allow him 'to decide whether he wishes to pursue his application in several countries at a time when, thanks to the international search report, he is in a better position to judge whether the expense of proceeding in those countries is justified'.[3]

The Treaty was signed by 35 states, the necessary number of ratifications have been made, and the treaty came into force in June 1978.

INTERNATIONAL PATENT CLASSIFICATION AGREEMENT (IPC) 1971
Covers 24 states (including the UK).

'The Treaty provides for the filing of an 'international application . . . containing particulars concerning the applicant, a reproduction of the mark, a list of the goods and/or services in connection with which the mark is used or is intended to be used, the designation of those of the contracting states in which protection of the mark is desired, and a request that the mark be registered in the International Register of Marks kept under the treaty by the International Bureau.'[3]

If the application complies with the treaty requirements, registration will be effected by the International Bureau, publication will be made in its Gazette and the contracting states involved will be notified. Each state will have a period of 15 months (18 months for Certification Trade Marks) in which recognition may be refused, otherwise the international registration will be equivalent to registration in each of the individual countries specified.

It is claimed that the main advantage of the TRT will be that the owner of the mark will 'obtain protection of his mark in several countries by filing only one application . . . in one language . . . and paying a single set of fees'.[3] It is said that renewal of the mark will also be 'particularly simple'.

The TRT is obviously similar to the Madrid Agreement (page 100). 'One of the main differences between the two is that under the Madrid Agreement only a mark registered in the national office of a contracting state may be registered internationally, whereas under the TRT no such previous national registration is required. Furthermore, under the Madrid Agreement, cancellation of the basic national registration during the first five years of the international registration entails cancellation of the international registration; such "dependence" does not exist under the TRT.'[3] There is also an arrangement whereby the owner of a registered mark is allowed 'considerable time for making the necessary preparations for use of the mark' in particular countries.

The treaty is not yet in force.

Establishes an international classification of the figurative elements of marks. The classification will consist of 29 categories, some 300 divisions and 3000 sections.

The agreement is not yet in force.

VIENNA AGREEMENT OF 1973

For the protection of type-faces and their international deposit.

The agreement is not yet in force.

BERNE COPYRIGHT CONVENTION OF 1886

For the protection of literary and artistic works.

As with the Paris Convention there is an International Union – the 'Berne Union' or the 'Copyright Union' – which comprises 68 states (including the UK). The United Kingdom has ratified the Brussels text (1948) but not the Paris text (1971). Notable non-members are the USA, USSR and the People's Republic of China.

The basic principles of the Berne Convention are, first, that 'works originating in one of the member states . . . must be given the same protection in each of the other member states as the latter grants to the works of its own nationals'; second, 'that such protection must not be conditional upon the complaince with any formality' – it must be automatic; and third that such protection will be independent of existing protection in the country of origin of the work. 'If, however, a country provides for a longer term than the minimum prescribed by the Convention and the work ceases to be protected in the country of origin, protection may be denied once protection in the country of origin ceases'.[3]

As to the Berne Convention's relevance to design, the Whitford Committee's report[2] says: 'the Paris text specifically states that the expression "literary and artistic works" shall include . . . works of drawing . . . works of applied art . . . and three-dimensional works relative to . . . architecture or science.' The report adds later that 'member states are . . . free to decide whether the protection to be given in the industrial design field shall be by copyright or special designs legislation or both. If such designs are protected by copyright then there is the possibility of automatic protection abroad.'

If, on the other hand, a Berne Convention country decides to cater for industrial designs exclusively under a registration procedure, then nationals of that country lose the right to claim automatic copyright protection abroad for their 'works of applied art'. The report concludes, as the explanation for one of the Committee's recommendations,

104

that if 'we wish to enjoy automatic copyright protection abroad for our "works of applied art", and to ratify the latest text of the Berne Convention, we shall have to give "applied art" designs a minimum period of 25 years from making.'[2]

The UK is a signatory and the latest text (1971) has also been ratified.

The UCC was created as 'a bridge between the United States of America, which was unwilling to join the Berne Convention, and the countries of Western Europe and the Western Alliance who were members'.[2] The standard of protection provided is lower than that of the Berne Copyright Convention. There are arrangements for collaboration with the Berne Union and with WIPO.

The UCC 'limits the formalities that any country may demand as a condition of protection to a notice of copyright on each published copy, being the symbol © with the year date of first publication and the name of the copyright owner'.[2]

DEVELOPMENTS IN EUROPE

Developments in Europe constitute an important part of the international position on design protection and they are particularly significant for manufacturers and designers in Britain. The move to co-operative action is more advanced in respect of patents than it is with trade marks or design registration or design copyright.

Many firms are obliged by the nature of their business to seek patent protection in many countries. Growing complexities in technology and the large number of patent applications in individual countries have led to a general slowing down in the patent-granting process. All of this has pointed to a clear need for action to reduce the great waste of time and money faced by manufacturers seeking international protection for inventions.

THE EUROPEAN PATENTS

In 1959 three working parties were set up by the EEC to seek 'harmonisation' between member countries in the whole field of protection for industrial property. This led in 1962 to a first draft for what is now known as the European Patent for the Common Market – 'the Community Patent'. In 1969 the then member countries extended their thinking to include non-member European states. The outcome was a Convention which established the European System for the Grant of Patents, with the European Patent Office (EPO) in Munich and a branch in The Hague which undertakes search for novelty. For a 15-year transition period, some of the work is entrusted to the British Patent Office in London. In addition to the nine members of the EEC there are other European signatories. The Convention which established the EPO came into force in 1977, patent applications being received from 1978. Patent protection is obtainable in all the contracting countries by a single application in one language English, French or German. The result is known as a 'bundle of national patents' – the 'bundle' being made up of the countries selected by the patentee for inclusion. As to cost the basis for a European patent should be about equal to the cost of patenting an invention separately in each of three of the member countries. With varying inflation rates between countries this cannot, however, be better than a guide.

The work of the EPO is related to the wider world of the Patent Co-operation Treaty (PCT) referred to on page 102. The PCT has, of course, similar objectives.

The aim for the Community Patent is even closer co-operation – 'to create a unitary Patent Law which will contribute towards the realisation of the objectives of the Treaty of Rome by eliminating, within the Community, the unequal conditions of competition and the obstacles to the free movement of goods which result from territorial limitations of national Patent Laws'.[5] The Community Patent Convention is not yet in force. When it does come into force the EPO will deal with applications for the grant of Community Patents but national patents will also continue.

A main reason for the British Patents Act 1977 was to bring British law into closer conformity with European and Community patent law plans.

TRADE MARKS

The second working party set up by the EEC in 1959 was charged with the task of seeking harmonisation in the field of trade marks. A Trade Mark Convention on the lines of the two European Patent Conventions was envisaged, but a press release from Brussels in 1976 was still stressing 'the necessity of creating an EEC Trade Mark as soon as possible' and emphasising 'the importance of an approximation of national laws as an accompanying measure'. 1979 was seen as a target date for a proposal to be submitted to the EEC Council.

There are British hopes that the European Trade Mark Office will be in London, but there is a counter claim by the French.

DESIGNS

The third working party was set up to deal with design. The Whitford Report says that 'it was originally proposed that a European Design Convention should be concluded . . . but no work has been done on it so far. The Commission, however, is under some pressure to take action in the field under their harmonisation programme since the measure of protection afforded in different member states varies greatly and this is a potential hindrance to intra-Community trade.'[2]

The final paragraph of the Committee's conclusions recognises that future legislation in Britain will be influenced by the 'likely pattern of design protection' in the EEC and goes on to make a plea 'to those likely to be engaged in formulating that pattern'.

'If a registration or deposit system is recommended for the more functional of designs, do not make such a system obligatory for all designs. Our reasons are: first we suspect an obligatory system will create as many problems as it solves; second because it is unsuitable (particularly if coupled with a requirement of novelty) for a number of trades; third because it is unrealistic to expect designers to register all their designs, particularly abroad and in more than one country. The great advantage of copyright internationally is simply that it is automatic. A Briton who writes a book or paints a picture enjoys automatic protection in most of the world. We urge that industrial designers should, in the case of (the more aesthetic) category A designs at least, enjoy the same advantage.'[2]

SOME INDIVIDUAL COUNTRIES

EUROPEAN COUNTRIES

Although there is strong pressure in Europe towards the development of a unified patent system, the countries of Europe at present exemplify the main difference in patent law between countries. Of the EEC countries, Italy, Belgium and Luxembourg, as distinct from Britain and the others, have simple patent registration systems – patents are granted without examination and search. A publication of the European Communities Commission[5] says that industry in such countries 'is placed at a disadvantage vis-a-vis large foreign firms which own a large number of unexamined patents and can make use of these patents in licence negotiations, without the national industry being in a position to assess the validity of the patents they are being offered'.

In France the patent system had been similar, but a Patents Act in 1968 introduced search for novelty—so many categories each year over a period of years—and by 1974 all patent applications became subject to search at the International Patent Institute at The Hague. A similar change has been suggested in Belgium.

As to designs, the French Copyright Act 1957 provides automatic protection in so far as the shape of the product is not dictated solely by function. 'The "level of creation and originality" is considered in determining whether or not copyright subsists in a design. Registered design protection is also available and there is protection, which can be far reaching, through the law of unfair competition.'[2]

The law in France (and in other countries) permits the registration of trade marks in respect of services ('service marks') as well as goods. As indicated on page 49 the Mathys Committee[16] recommended in 1974 that we should make the change and register service marks in the UK. French trade mark law also allows for registration of the distinctive shape and appearance of articles, including containers of products.

There is a bilateral trade mark treaty between France and Italy. Trade marks of nationals registered in one country are recognised in the other on payment of an extra fee.

In West Germany, the Copyright Law of 1965 extends protection to 'works of applied art'. 'The subjective determination of whether or not there is a "sufficient level of artistic creation" or "personal intellectual creation" for copyright to subsist in a work is left to the courts to decide.' From case law so far, it seems 'that useful items can enjoy copyright protection as works of applied art if they are clearly distinguishable from shapes already known and if such comparison with what is already known' points to a 'considerable creative accomplishment'.[2]

In Germany the normal copyright term is for life plus 70 years, compared with life plus 50 in the UK. Drawings, being works of art, are protected against reproduction as drawings but they do not provide a basis of protection for industrially produced products.

There is also protection for designs in Germany by registration but the system is closer to patent law than it is in Britain. Protection is for 15 years and revision of the law is being considered. 'In addition, the law of unfair competition provides a measure of protection in appropriate cases, eg if there is confusion as to trade source (passing off).'[2]

Patent law in Holland, as distinct from the other two Benelux countries, is noted for the rigorous nature of the search required, but in Holland, Belgium and Luxembourg there is now a unified design law, which has been effective since 1975. There is design protection for 'the new appearance of a product having a utility function', but excluded from this is 'anything indispensable for the achievement of a technical result'. Some difficult categories of products are specifically excluded. The system is based on design registration; there is a requirement for novelty for which the criteria are defined but there is no official search. The designs registered are published.

'Dual protection (registration and copyright) is specifically envisaged for designs having a "marked artistic character". However, unless a specific declaration is made for the continuation of the copyright or unless the rights are held by different proprietors, the copyright in the design will normally lapse together with the right in the registered design. Protection under unfair competition legislation is not available if registration of a design has not been applied for.'[2]

On the subject of moral rights, and with copyright in general in mind (but including design), the report of the Whitford Committee[2] refers in approving terms to the recently revised Netherlands Copyright Act. The Act provides for the author to retain certain rights 'even after transfer of his copyright' including: 'the right to object to publication of the work under a name other than his own...' and 'the right to object to any distortion, mutilation or other modification of the work which would be prejudicial to the honour or reputation of the author...' This right is limited in respect of modifications 'where the nature of the modification is such that it would be unreasonable to object to it'.[35]

In Scandinavia there is a unified system having some similarity to that in the Benelux countries. Denmark, Norway, Sweden and Finland adopted laws in the early 1970s whereby 'articles are protected irrespective of whether the shape of the article is conditioned by technical or aesthetic reasons. A limited number of designs are protected by copyright law as well.' [2]

AUSTRALIA AND NEW ZEALAND

In Australia and New Zealand patent and trade mark law is similar to that in Britain (for patents, prior to the 1977 Act). Australian protection for industrial designs, however, is only by registration and 'automatic copyright protection under the Australian Copyright Act 1968 ceases as soon as a design is applied industrially or is registered'.[2] A review committee in 1973 recommended a rather broader definition of design for the purpose of protection by registration, but was against copyright protection except for 'two-dimensional pattern or ornament applicable to the surface of an article'.[2] The recommendations have not as yet been enacted.

Design protection in New Zealand is closer to that in Britain. There is design registration in parallel with protection by design copyright. Design copyright is, however, for the full term of life plus 50 years.

CANADA

Patent law in Canada is also similar to British law before the 1977 Patents Act. Search is normally limited to prior Canadian patents, but other inventions whose publication in other countries anticipated the patent applied for may be cited against grant of the patent. Applications for patents are not published or open to inspection before the patent is granted.

Canada has a design registration system, novelty in respect of appearance being a requirement rather than functional or constructional characteristics. Nevertheless, designs are accepted for registration when in some other countries they would be thought of as 'utility models'.

Trade mark law admits goods and services for registration; also products of distinctive appearance including product containers and packaging.

UNITED STATES OF AMERICA

The USA is probably the most patent-conscious country in the world. American patents are given after careful examination and search, and American firms take out great numbers of patents in virtually every country in the world.

The Whitford Report comments that 'there is little effective protection for industrial designs or mechanical drawings as such under American copyright law' and continues 'Designs are mainly catered for by a design patent system which not only requires a design to involve an ornamental appearance but also demands "invention".'[2]

An American author[36] describes the copyright system by saying that 'if the appearance of a utilitarian article contains "artistic features" which can be identified separately and exist independently, those features, in many cases, may be copyrighted'. Apart from books, plays, films, music etc, copyright also applies to maps; works of art; reproductions of works of art; technical and scientific drawings and models; photographs; prints and pictorial illustrations, and commercial prints or labels.

A new copyright law came into force in 1978. Prior to this registration had been necessary for copyright protection in the US. This is no longer so, but registration is still 'a prerequisite for all infringement suits. This means that if someone, after the fact, infringes your work, you can still go ahead and register your copyright and then sue'. There are provisions respecting 'fair use' as a limitation on copyright owners'. As to marking, the previous legal requirement was for material for which copyright was claimed, to carry the symbol © or other copyright indications together with the year of publication and the name of the copyright owner or abbreviations in some cases. 'The new law also calls for notices but provides that omissions or errors will not immediately result in forfeiture of rights.'

Trade marks in the US relate to both goods and services. 'Rights to own trade marks are provided under common law, and as such, do not depend on federal statutes for legitimacy so federal registration is not required. Nevertheless, there is potential value in filing for registration. By doing so you establish formal notice of your claim to ownership. This supports your valid and exclusive right to use a mark in defense of potential infringement claims.'[34]

JAPAN

The Japanese patent system has similarities to current British law, publication being made in the *Patent Gazette* 18 months after application, irrespective of the position as regards examination and search. A written request for examination (which is thorough) may, however, be made by the applicant for the patent or by a third party at any time within 7 years. If no request is made within that time the application for a patent is deemed to have been withdrawn.

There is a system of protection for 'utility models' which is related to patent law. A utility model is defined as any novel device that can be used industrially and that relates to the shape, construction or method of assembly of an article. There is also protection for designs by registration, the principal test being novelty. Japan is a signatory of the Berne Copyright Convention.

Trade mark registration is restricted to goods as distinct from services. The Japanese do not have the equivalent of a Certification Trade Mark system. Marking is not compulsory but it is advisable. The indication of registration is given by the Japanese ideographs for 'Registered Trade Mark'.

THE USSR (SOVIET UNION)
'In the Soviet Union and a few other countries, inventors may apply either for patents or for inventors' certificates. Under the latter, the exclusive right to the invention belongs to the State, but the inventor has a right to appropriate remuneration as well as certain other rights and privileges.'[3] Inventors living in the USSR almost always apply for inventors' certificates (more generally known as 'authorship certificates'). For foreign firms a patent will obviously be more appropriate. There is a similar situation as regards designs or 'industrial models'. Design patents or certificates of authorship are both possible. An industrial design is defined as being a new artistic formulation of an article suitable for industrial production in which technical and aesthetic qualities are combined.

The USSR is a member of the Paris Union (Paris Convention for the Protection of Industrial Property) but not of the Berne Union (Berne Copyright Convention). Most of the Eastern European countries are members of both.

The USSR law in respect of trade marks reads very similarly to that of a Western country. Service marks are registrable as well as marks for goods. Particularly distinctive forms of packaging may also be registered.

Appendix

Extract from the Report of the Committee to consider the Law on Copyright and Designs 1977, Chairman The Hon Mr Justice Whitford. (The references are to paragraphs and chapters in the report. The proposed categories A and B for designs are explained on page 37 of this book.)

SUMMARY OF RECOMMENDATIONS

Chapter 3
Industrial designs

923 In relation to designs consisting only of surface pattern and the shapes of three-dimensional articles of which the aesthetic appearance will influence a purchaser in making a purchase (referred to as category A designs—see paragraph 167):

1 At least the aesthetic elements of these designs should be given protection in respect of their appearance (but not in respect of any underlying idea or principle) under the general law of copyright, without the formality of registration or deposit. All but two of the Committee would in fact recommend protection for the design viewed as a whole, subject to the understanding that copyright protection does not, in the case of any design, protect the underlying idea or principle (paragraph 180).

2 The term of protection, once the design has been industrially applied, should be 25 years from marketing (paragraph 181).

3 To ensure adequate notice of the claim to protection, damages should not be recoverable in respect of infringement committed before specific notice of the claim to copyright or unless notice has been given by way of marking on the article or, where this is not possible, on the packaging for the article or literature issued with the article (paragraph 181).

924 In relation to designs comprising the shapes of three-dimensional articles where the appearance of the article does not influence the purchaser, who buys the article only in the expectation that it will do the job for which it is intended (referred to as category B designs—see paragraph 168), the Committee is divided:

1 Two members would exclude category B designs from copyright protection altogether (paragraph 185).

2 Four members would give category B designs the same protection as the majority recommended for category A, and on the same basis (paragraph 192).

3 Three members would protect category B designs only under a design deposit copyright system for a period of protection between 15 and 25 years, on the basis recommended by the Johnston Committee. Deposit should not be refused on the grounds that it is a category A design, nor should deposit amount to an admission that it is not such a design (paragraph 192).

925 Other recommendations relating to industrial designs:

1 Registered design monopoly protection, as now provided by the Registered Designs Act 1949, should be repealed, but subject, in the view of two members, to the introduction of a design deposit system providing a satisfactory alternative basis for claims to priority overseas under the Paris Industrial Property Convention (paragraph 193).

2 Copyright should subsist in original works which start their life in three dimensions, as well as in two, whether or not these could now be described as works of sculpture or 'works of artistic craftsmanship' (paragraph 197).

3 In the case of category B designs (paragraph 924), it should be possible to obtain compulsory licences on the ground that the United Kingdom market is not being adequately supplied by manufacture within the Community (paragraph 194).

4 The Crown should have equivalent powers to those it now enjoys as regards registered designs under Schedule 1 to the Registered Designs Act 1949 (paragraph 195).

5 The present position as regards term of artistic works (such as drawings) should be continued, ie that they

should have protection as such for the life of the author plus 50 years (paragraph 196).

6 Certain works of an artistic character should continue to retain full copyright protection even after mass-production, as now provided for in the rules made under Section 1(4) of the Registered Designs Act 1949 (paragraph 196).

7 Section 9(8) of the Copyright Act 1956, which postulates a 'non-expert' test, should be repealed (paragraph 197).

8 Convention nationals should not enjoy automatic copyright protection (ie protection without deposit) for their designs in the United Kingdom unless they enjoy such protection for the same designs in their own countries (paragraph 197).

9 There should be a statutory prohibition in respect of unjustified threats of proceedings for infringement of copyright over the whole field of copyright, but not in respect of threats made to the primary infringer (paragraph 198).

926 In Chapter 15 there are recommendations for the abolition of the provisions for pecuniary remedies in respect of conversion and detention contained in Section 18 of the Copyright Act 1956, but the retention of a discretionary remedy of delivery up. It is also recommended there that the remedies against infringers of industrial designs should be the same as are recommended should be available in future against infringers in any other copyright field. The question of copyright in the drawings of patent specifications is considered in Chapter 19.

References

1 *Report of the Departmental Committee on Industrial Designs 1962* Chairman, Mr Kenneth Johnston QC, HMSO

2 *Report of the Committee to consider the Law on Copyright and Designs 1977* Chairman, The Hon Mr Justice Whitford, HMSO

3 *General Information World Intellectual Property Organisation 1977* WIPO Publication

4 *Inaugural Address* by Lord Nathan, Royal Society of Arts 1976, RSA

5 *European Patent* Commission of the European Communities, 1973 European Communities Commission UK Office

6 *Applying for a Patent* The Patent Office

7 *Patents Act 1977* HMSO

8 *Protection of Industrial Designs* The Patent Office

9 *Russell-Clarke on Copyright in Industrial Designs fifth edition* Michael Fysh, Sweet and Maxwell

10 *Design Copyright Bill* Board of Trade press notice 1968

11 Dorling v Honnor Marine Ltd and another 1964

12 Amp Inc v Utilux Proprietory Ltd 1972

13 George Hensher Ltd v Restawhile Upholstery (Lancs) Ltd 1974

14 *Applying for a Trade Mark* The Patent Office

15 *Patents, Trade Marks, Copyright and Industrial Designs* T A Blanco White and Robin Jacob, Sweet and Maxwell

16 *Report of the Committee to examine British Trade Mark Law and Practice 1974* Chairman – Mr H R Mathys, HMSO

17 *Design Plagiarism and Copyright Reform* lecture by A D Russell-Clarke to the Royal Society of Arts 1968, RSA

18 *Letter of Assignment of Design* Wallcovering Manufacturers Association of Great Britain, 1977

19 *Society of Industrial Artists and Designers Code of Professional Conduct* SIAD

20 *The Professional Practice of Design* Dorothy Goslett, Batsford, revised edition, 1978

21 'The Designerr and the Law – a historical perspective' Dr Mary Vitoria in *Design History – Fad or Function?* Design Council, 1978

22 *Patents and Income Tax No 490* Board of Inland Revenue, 1964

23 *Income and Corporation Taxes Act 1970* sections 389–392 HMSO

24 Blair v Osborne and Tomkins 1970

25 Stovin-Bradford v Volpoint Properties Ltd 1971

26 *Royal Institute of British Architects Conditions of Engagement* RIBA, 1971

27 *Society of Industrial Artists and Designers Yearbook 1976/77* SIAD

28 *Submission of evidence to the Departmental Committee to consider the Law on Copyright and Designs, SIAD, 1974* SIAD

29 LB (Plastics) Ltd v Swish Products Ltd 1977

30 *Assay Office* Goldsmiths' Hall, London

31 King Features Syndicate Inc and Betts v O and M Kleeman Ltd 1941

32 Burke and Margo Burke Ltd v Spicers Dress Designs 1936

33 Radley Gowns Ltd v Costas Spyrou 1975

34 Lerose Ltd v Hawick Jersey International Ltd 1974

35 *Netherlands Copyright Act* 1912, revised 1972, Article 25

36 Larry Bell, Associate Professor of Industrial Design, University of Illinois *Industrial Design* Sept/Oct 1977

Organisations concerned with design protection

Chartered Institute of Patent Agents
Staple Inn Buildings
London WC1V 7PZ

European Communities Commission UK Office
20 Kensington Palace Gardens
London W8 QQ

Design Council
28 Haymarket
London SW1Y 4SU

Designs Registry
at the Patent Office, London
and at Baskerville House
Browncross Street
New Bailey Street
Salford M3 5FU

Fashion Design Protection Asociation
27 Broadley Terrace
London NW1 6LG

Institute of Trade Mark Agents
69 Cannon Street
London EC4N 5AB

The Law Society
113 Chancery Lane
London WC2A 1PL

Patent Office
25 Southampton Buildings
London WC2A 1AY

Royal Institute of British Architects
66 Portland Place
London W1N 4AD

Society of Industrial Artists and Designers
Nash House
12 Carlton House Terrace
London SW1Y 5AH

Trade Marks Registry
at the Patent Office, London
and at Baskerville House
Browncross Street
New Bailey Street
Salford M3 5FU

World Intellectual Property Organisation
32 chemin des Columbettes
1211 Geneva 20
Switzerland

Worshipful Company of Goldsmiths
Assay Office
Goldsmiths' Hall
Gutter Lane
London EC2V 8AQ

Index